Dunc[an ...]
P[lays]

Julie Allardyce, One [Sure Thing,]
Shuv, Blackden, [...]

'Duncan McLean has an uncomfortably clear eye, able to watch without flinching or passing judgement. From the mouths of his characters come all the passing cruelty and absurdity, the daftness and awfulness that make up so-called ordinary communication. Lean, maggoty, subversively funny; Scottish and universal; these plays are genuine, tooth-bitten gold.'
Janice Galloway

Julie Allardyce: 'Here is a play which makes us feel and see what it is like to work offshore on those strange iron prisons with their unsettling combination of five-star services and social deprivation ... *Julie Allardyce* rushes into the theatre like a fresh breeze off the North Sea. It is loud and coarse-tongued and funny, a series of affectionate but telling snapshots which add up to a revealing portrait of the north-east as it is now ... a play which opens doors and shoves the audience through into areas of new experience.' *Scotland on Sunday*

Blackden: 'McLean's adaptation of his own text is, in fact, something of a revelation, a tribute to the kind of intense, plastic reworking that can take place when a young, gifted novelist who is also a playwright is given a chance to revisit his own material ... The result is a gripping, ominous meditation on the strange disappearance of a young man in his prime, driven along by the hard, powerful lilt of McLean's Aberdeenshire Scots ... The deep-rooted strength of McLean's language and characterisation – and the compelling 1990s significance of the themes he grapples with – sex and masculinity, identity and kinship, aspiration, culture and the ties that bind – wins through, exerting a hold on the audience that deepens into rapt attention, as the story spirals towards its strange, unresolved ending.' *Scotland on Sunday*

Also included are three short pieces, *Rug Comes to Shuv* ('nasty, brutish and hilarious ... with unexpectedly poignant undercurrents' *The Scotsman*), *One Sure Thing* and *I'd Rather Go Blind*.

Duncan McLean was born in Aberdeenshire in 1964. In the eighties he was a writer and performer with the Merry Mac Fun Co, a co-operative which toured Scotland. His plays include *One Sure Thing* (1992), *Julie Allardyce* (1993), *The Horseman's Word* (1995), *Rug Comes to Shuv* (1996), *Blackden* (1997), and *I'd Rather Go Blind* (1999). His other works include a book of short stories, *Bucket of Tongues*, which won the Somerset Maugham Award in 1993; two novels, *Blackden* (1994) and *Bunker Man* (1995); and *Lone Star Swing*, which won a Scottish Arts Council Book Award in 1998. He is editor of The Clocktower Press and lives in Orkney.

DUNCAN McLEAN

Plays: 1

Julie Allardyce
One Sure Thing
Rug Comes to Shuv
Blackden
I'd Rather Go Blind

introduced by the author

Methuen Drama

METHUEN CONTEMPORARY DRAMATISTS

1 3 5 7 9 10 8 6 4 2

This collection first published in the United Kingdom in 1999 by
Methuen Publishing Limited
215 Vauxhall Bridge Road, London SW1V 1EJ

Peribo Pty Ltd, 58 Beaumont Road, Mount Kuring-Gai,
NSW 2080, Australia, ACN 002 273 761
(for Australia and New Zealand)

Julie Allardyce first published in *Theatre Scotland*, Autumn 1993
This revised version first published by Methuen Drama in 1995
Copyright © 1993, 1995 by Duncan McLean
One Sure Thing, Rug Comes to Shuv,
Blackden and *I'd Rather Go Blind* first published in this edition
One Sure Thing copyright © 1999 by Duncan McLean
Rug Comes to Shuv copyright © 1999 by Duncan McLean
Blackden copyright © 1999 by Duncan McLean
I'd Rather Go Blind copyright © 1999 by Duncan McLean

Introduction and collection copyright © 1999 by Duncan McLean

The right of the author to be identified as the translator of these works has
been asserted by him in accordance with the Copyright, Designs and
Patents Act, 1988

Methuen Publishing Limited Reg. No. 3543167

A CIP catalogue record for this book
is available from the British Library

ISBN 0 413 72900 1

Typeset by Deltatype Ltd, Birkenhead, Merseyside
Printed and bound in Great Britain by
Cox & Wyman Ltd, Reading, Berks

Contents

Duncan McLean
Chronology

Plays

1985   *The Ran-Dan* directed by Beth Twist, Merry
       Mac Fun Co (touring Edinburgh and Glasgow)
1986   *Sharny Dubs* directed by Ben Twist, Merry Mac
       Fun Co (touring throughout Scotland)
1987   *The Country Doctor* directed by Ben Twist, Merry
       Mac Fun Co (touring throughout Scotland)
1990   *4 Goblin Hamburgers in Gravy* directed by Duncan
       McLean, Pilton Triangle Arts Centre,
       Edinburgh
1990   *Two Young Fuckers* directed by Ben Twist, Pilton
       Triangle Arts Centre, Edinburgh
1992   *One Sure Thing* directed by Steve Crone,
       Castlemilk People's Theatre, Glasgow
1993   *Julie Allardyce* directed by Paul Pinson,
       Boilerhouse Theatre Company/The Lemon
       Tree, Aberdeen
1995   *The Horseman's Word* directed by Dave Grieve,
       St Magnus Festival, Orkney
1996   *Rug Comes to Shuv* directed by John Tiffany,
       Traverse Theatre, Edinburgh
1997   *Blackden* directed by Peter Mackie Burns,
       Castlemilk People's Theatre, Glasgow
1998   *Rug Comes to Shuv* (translated by Jean-Michel
       Déprats) directed by Eleonora Rossi, Théâtre
       Gérard Philipe, Saint-Denis, Paris
1999   *I'd Rather Go Blind* directed by Philip Howard,
       Traverse Theatre, Edinburgh and on tour

Fiction and non-fiction

1992   *Bucket of Tongues* (short stories), winner of the
       Somerset Maugham Award in 1993

1994   *Blackden* (novel)
1995   *Bunker Man* (novel)
1997   *Lone Star Swing: On the Trail of Bob Wills and his Texas Playboys* (travel/music), winner of a Scottish Arts Council Book Award in 1998
1997   Editor of *Ahead of its Time: A Clocktower Press Anthology*

TV

1992   *The Doubles* (short drama for Greenwich Films/BBC 2)
1995   *Sittin' on Top of the World* (documentary on Texas music and Scottish writing for BBC2)
1996   *Family Butcher* (screenplay – unproduced)

Introduction
Getting an Edge

Brecht's poem, 'On Everyday Theatre', argues that the most powerful form of theatre is that embodied by ordinary people – pub yarners, flirting youths – when they're bursting to share some story with the folk around them. Take the witness to a road accident, for instance. See the minimal body movements showing the swerve of the car, the sound effects generated in the throat or by the slapping of fist against palm, the inflexion or accentuation of the voice to imitate the driver's gasp, the cry of the man knocked over . . . Brecht calls it 'everyday, thousandfold, fameless / But vivid'.

Of course the listeners gathered round the street corner would never believe the witness actually *was* the driver, or his victim. That's not what anyone requires. The witness wants to convey the detail and drama of what he's just seen; the crowd wants to understand what's happened, who's to blame – and maybe they want to share vicariously in that adrenalin-pumping moment when the car came swerving across the pavement. 'Jesus, you should've seen it!' says the witness. And through him they do.

When I first read that poem it affected me greatly. Not because it was a revelation, a fresh idea, but because it expressed so clearly what I already believed. Christ, I thought I'd worked out the notion of Street Corner Theatre for myself, but here was one of the world's best-known writers beating me to it by fifty-five years.

I studied drama at university and had good teachers, but the best teacher of all was (of course) experience. From the start of 1985, for three solid years, I was a member of a comedy trio (and occasional quartet) called The Merry Mac Fun Show. We performed our songs and patter in just about every venue imaginable: from youth clubs and unemployed workers' centres to night-clubs and student unions, from theatres in the West End of London to church halls and pillbox pubs on run-down housing estates. We performed street theatre in Edinburgh in and out of the Festival, in Glasgow on the day of the 1987 Scotland v. England football match, and in Covent Garden's piazza in front of anything from 3 to 3,000 people. We haunted the studios of Scotland's local radio stations, and appeared on *Wogan* with Selina Scott, Billy Bragg and Eddie Shah.

All this gigging in all these different places taught me that there are really just two things that are truly, ultimately, crucially necessary for theatre: the audience and the performer. Everything else – lights, props, make-up, scenery, music, interval drinks and ice cream, fancy costumes, proscenium arches, thrust stages, trap-doors, dry-ice machines and post-show discussions – everything else is unnecessary. Added attractions at best, terrible distractions very often.

Street theatre is where I learned all my most important lessons, so of course I believe it to be the best possible education for a would-be playwright. There's nothing in theatre to beat the terror and exhilaration of stepping out into a Saturday shopping street or a miners' gala armed with nothing but a sore throat, a battered guitar, and a series of jokes about the Department of Social Security. No prompter to feed you lines, no lights to make you look pretty, no comfy seats and darkened aisles to keep the punters in their seats till at least half time. All there is is you and the audience, and the gap between the two of you. And what you have to do is reach across the gap immediately, bridge it, grab the audience. Because until you grab them there *is* no audience – there are only passers-by. You grab the passers-by and *make them into* an audience.

Buskers call it 'getting an edge': that magic moment when the two or three folk slowing as they pass turn into a dozen wondering whether to stay or not, who turn into twenty standing, staring, laughing. They become an audience. The edge defines a performance area. You're no longer speaking or singing to yourself: you're making theatre.

Looking over these plays as a group, it's pretty clear to me that I'm still trying to get an edge, even though all these pieces were written to be performed away from the thrill and fear of the street pitch, in more or less conventional theatre buildings. What I'm after is still that direct and immediate contact with the audience. I want my plays to grab them from the first second and keep them grabbed.

Am I worried that the audience is going to get up and walk out if I don't hold them by the lapels? Maybe. There's more to it than that though. I've only got ninety minutes to tell the stories I'm bursting to tell – in fact, in the case of the short plays, I've got more like fifteen minutes. I've no time to waste. The kebab shop and the late-night video call. Urgency is all.

Urgency. If you're not filled with urgency when you're writing a play you're in the wrong medium. Go home and write a letter instead. Write 200 letters, and send them individually to everyone who would've been your audience. Better still, write a good long novel: 500 pages take even a fast reader several days to get through.

There's space in a novel for the author to indulge in digressions, background colour, multiple sub-plots; there's time for the reader to go back and reread, to refresh their memory, to compare and contrast. But theatre's not like that. Every show is an organic whole: the edge forms in the opening seconds and stays there. The performance grows like a bubble of gum, bigger and bigger, always intact. It has to stay intact: if the audience's attention wanders and the bubble bursts you're left with a mucky face. In street terms, if the edge breaks up you're not making theatre any more; you're just talking to yourself.

Allow me now to risk talking to myself for a few moments, and say a few words about each of these plays in turn.

The thing that really got me excited about the commission to write *Julie Allardyce* was that it allowed me to write about the north-east, and for north-east actors; most importantly, it meant the play would have a decent run of performances in the area's capital, Aberdeen. None of my previous plays had stayed in Aberdeenshire for more than a few nights before moving on, so I was keen to make the most of this opportunity to create something specifically for the place I come from.

Initially, we discussed my writing a play about the impact of the oil industry on the north-east. Before long the emphasis, quite rightly, shifted: this was to be a play about the *people* of the north-east, not about 'impact' or any other abstract notion. But I certainly couldn't ignore the oil: I knew from my own experience – and that of my friends and family – that everyone who lives within fifty miles of Aberdeen has their lives affected by the oil every day, whether they like to admit it or not. I felt this to be particularly true of folk of my own age group, whose birth coincided with the discovery of North Sea oil, who have grown up alongside the industry, and whose notion of their identity is far less fixed and certain than that of their immediate ancestors.

My first task in writing the script was to find a character who was typical or representative of this oil generation – somebody born in the mid-sixties or later – who had no memory of the pre-oil days, who'd been brought up surrounded by, and often taking for granted, the high-tech multinational-capitalist culture that comes along with the oil companies. But somebody who was not *so* far removed from traditional work and life of the north-east that they couldn't feel the pull of the old ways in their bones from time to time. In his trilogy of novels, *A Scots Quair*, set in the Mearns to the south of Aberdeen, Lewis Grassic Gibbon created such a character for the years around the first world war: Chris Guthrie. The *Quair* is one of the great books of the century, and my own much less ambitious and inspired effort can only suffer by comparison to it. But I feel I must mention Gibbon because I'm sure his example had a lot to do with the way I came to imagine *my* central character, Julie Allardyce.

While I'm owning up to influences, I should mention a less obvious but probably more important one: Kasimir Malevich, the Ukrainian Suprematist painter. An exhibition of avant-garde art from the years around the Russian Revolution visited Edinburgh in the summer of 1993, and I was immediately excited by the work of Malevich and his contemporaries, especially Liubov Popova and Olga Rosanova. I was very struck by Malevich's paintings such as *Suprematist Painting: Aeroplane Flying* and *Black Square and Red Square* (both 1915). I loved their clean, sharp lines, and the way the different rectangles and crosses and circles of bright colour floated apart from each other: untouching, but in harmony.

As I wrote *Julie Allardyce*, I found myself attempting to create the dramatic equivalent of a Suprematist painting. Different scenes emerged in different styles – naturalism, folktale-telling, stand-up comedy, Brechtian epic, *son-et-lumière*, bothy nicht . . . you spot them. My feeling was that life in the north-east these days is fragmented, with bits of old traditional local culture, bits of culture from Europe, Japan, America; people born in all parts of the globe have settled there, and locals go off to work and live in the Middle East and Texas; some folk think oil has been a curse on the way of life in the area, others that oil saved the north-east from becoming an economic disaster area. I believed it would be fitting to imitate this kaleidoscope of experience in the very form of the play. More than that: I thought I would be ignoring the reality of life in the area if I didn't attempt to write a drama of contrasting – but ultimately harmonious – scenes, textures, styles.

I wanted the styles of acting to change from scene to scene. I wanted the lighting to drench each scene in different bright colours, or in darkness. I wanted a soundtrack of delicate fiddle music and brutal industrial noise. I wanted a set of big, bold geometric shapes, echoing both the paintings of Malevich and also the (strangely Suprematist) sights to be seen around Aberdeen harbour: huge blue cranes with yellow jibs, bright red support vessels and orange lifeboats, enormous rectangular sheds along the quays, ferries in blue, white and orange with ten-foot-high lettering on their sides, squads of circular tanks for oil and gas storage. And the green links, the yellow beach, the grey sea and the black black oil.

In other words, I felt that the stories I was bursting to tell about the north-east could be told best, that the audience could be grabbed quickest and held onto most firmly, by using this kaleidoscopic approach.

One Sure Thing was written for Castlemilk People's Theatre, to be part of an evening of short plays called *Four Funerals and a Wedding*. It's more or less an adaptation of my earlier story 'Dying and Being Alive'. I'd written (and performed) innumerable direct-address comedy pieces – stand-up routines, parodic rants, character monologues – but this was more or less my first attempt to use the form for something serious. What I found interesting in writing this piece was the layering effect that comes with a first-person monologue. You have the layer of immediate drama – the character standing and talking to you – then you have a once-removed layer – where the character acts out scenes from his memory or imagination. Switching back and forth between the two brings interesting contrasts, even contradictions. If the character senses these contradictions, that's a third layer, but I don't think Keith in *One Sure Thing* got that far. (The audience did.) In *Blackden* I would go on to explore further the possibilities of the monologue.

By the way, the question 'What's the one sure thing?' (with the answer as given in the play) was a favourite one of Miss Ella Bowman, who taught us English when I was about thirteen. Why she thought this would help us understand *The Merchant of Venice* better, I still don't know.

I sometimes wonder whether my use of recorded music as

an integral part of my plays would be different, or there at all, if I'd had the chance to have original music, performed live. *Julie Allardyce* had specially commissioned music, but it was never live: Ken Slaven recorded it on tape and the tape was played each night. Apart from that, the companies I've written for have never been able to afford a pit band or a composer. Instead, I've made the most of what was possible, and written specific classic records into my scripts. As Dennis Potter and his uncle pointed out long ago, there's nothing quite so evocative of a mood as the right piece of popular music.

It was a thrill for me to sit in the audience the first time *Rug Comes to Shuv* was played, and feel the audience thrill as the opening track by Primal Scream pounded out. I could see them sit up straighter, focus on the stage, prick up their ears for what was about to burst onto the stage: I'd grabbed them, Primal Scream had got me an edge. The French translation of this play used the same music, but the director came up with a few other ideas to hook the audience from the opening moments. She had a projector set up to beam excerpts from old cartoon films onto the back wall of the theatre: mostly cats and dogs beating each other up, but also people getting squashed by steamrollers, hammers flattening heads, and various random images and blobs of colour. The characters didn't pay any attention to the projections, but the audience did. And I did!

I know a few playwrights who would be appalled to the point of walking out (causing as much disruption as possible on the way) if any director pulled a stunt like that, but I welcome such bold interventions. I'm not a hundred per cent convinced that it worked – Rug and Shuv are humans, not drawings, and I wouldn't like any audience to think otherwise – but I am a hundred per cent sure it made for a very exciting piece of theatre. In fact Eleonora Rossi's *Rug Comes to Shuv* was just about the best production of any of 'my' plays I've seen: a very good edge.

Blackden was a further exploration of the possibilities of the monologue, beyond *One Sure Thing*. Except, as I said earlier, I'd been writing comedy monologues for years before that. So although I'm aware of the interesting work of Brian Friel and Alan Bennett and many others in this form, I was probably more influenced by people like Dario Fo or even Jerry Sadowitz: two great writers outside the confines of conventional theatre, whose inimitable performances and utter commitment to their vision still inspire me. If there were Nobel prizes for Card Magic or for Scathing, Scatological, Satirical Stand-up, then Sadowitz would get my vote any day.

Peter Mackie Burns made a fine job of directing *Blackden* at the Tron in Glasgow. He made a few significant changes from how I'd envisaged the staging of the play. For instance, he did away with the notion of the characters sitting in the audience and stepping up onto the stage when it came their turn to speak. I'd suggested this because I wanted the whole play to feel like an evening of stories: a group of friends or acquaintances who've chanced to meet and take the opportunity to pore over the strange disappearance of their neighbour Patrick Hunter. I didn't want there to be Audience and Actors; I just wanted a bunch of folk sitting around, some of whom happen to speak, and some of whom (for this eighty minutes at least) happen not to. Again I was striving for that direct contact between the performers and the audience: the unmediated sharing of stories and memories. Peter didn't think that all of my suggestions for achieving this direct contact worked and so he came up with his own. Fair enough: I wouldn't object to *Blackden* being performed by a troupe of nude trapeze artists if the director thought that Brian and the others swinging through the air without a sequin in sight would make the most immediate contact.

Blackden was a novel before it was a play, but anyone who reads both will find that the latter is not a straightforward staging of the former. Partly this was because I would have been bored to tears by having to plod through the book changing 'said Brian's into **Brian**s and cutting half the characters and stories. Mostly, though, it was because the form and tone that (I hope) establish contact between the narrator and the reader in the novel just would not work on the stage. I had to find another way of telling the story. So I stuck the book back on the shelf and started from scratch. (What I'm really trying to say is, just because you've read the play, don't feel you can't go out and buy the novel too . . .)

I'd Rather Go Blind is the most recent play here; indeed, as I write this, it has not yet started rehearsals. It seems to me that it draws on the approaches of both my monologue plays and my supercharged dialogue plays (such as *Rug Comes to Shuv*, or *4 Goblin Hamburgers in Gravy*, not included here). I've tried to blend these two approaches before, in a play called *Two Young Fuckers*, which started off with a vicious argument between two desperate characters and ended forty minutes later with a long demented rant by the nominal winner of the argument. I was dissatisfied with that piece in various ways and have decided not to print or restage it; but the approach I explored there seemed a potentially fruitful one to me and I have tried it again in this short play – and hope to do so at length sometime.

In conclusion, allow me to state the bleeding obvious. *I'd Rather Go Blind* is both parody of and tribute to the kind of pseudo-therapeutic, genuinely-voyeuristic chat shows so popular on TV these past few years. Jerry Springer's show is the best (or, to put it another way, the worst) of these. He, and other hosts, have lately been criticised because at least some of their guests, and some of the punch-ups they get into, have been revealed to be fakes. Big deal. *Macbeth* was fake! That wasn't real history! See when Macbeth and Malcolm had their big fight at the end? That wasn't real: that was two actors waving wooden swords about. And fake blood! And when that woman took her clothes off and wandered about wringing her hands? She wasn't really mad, she'd been given those lines by some cheap hack in the production office.

Yes folks, if Shakespeare was alive today he'd be writing for Ricki Lake.

And why not? What were all those soliloquies but the Elizabethan way of getting direct access to the powerful emotions and twisted thoughts of Hamlet and the rest of them? Now we don't need soliloquies: you just sit your prince down in front of a TV camera, a baying audience, and a shamelessly probing host, and he pours it all out . . . 'Aye, well, like I say Ricki, I wasn't really nuts, I was just putting it on to get back at my uncle, cause he was shagging my mother see. But it kind of got out of control, ken, and before I knew it my girlfriend was *really* off her trolley . . .'

Different writers and performers at different times have come up with different ways of getting an edge. This book includes a few of my attempts to date. In so far as any of them succeed, a lot of credit must go to all the actors, directors and others who helped me shape them. Above all, I'd like to greet and salute my two main comrades from the Merry Mac days, John McKay and Jez Benstock:

Here's tae ye, wha's like ye?
Damn few, an they're aa deid!

Duncan McLean
Orkney, 1999

Julie Allardyce

Characters

Julie Allardyce, *twenty-two, ROV operator, originally from near Fyvie*
David Mitchell, *going out with Julie, roustabout, Aberdonian*
Finn Finlay, *from a southern Scottish city, another ROV operator*
Gary Grant, *operations – 'ops' – controller on the rig*
Angela Bruce, *Julie's best friend since school, unemployed, with a young kid*
Drew Allardyce, *Julie's brother, a couple of years older than her, works the family farm*

Julie Allardyce was first performed at The Lemon Tree, West North Street, Aberdeen, on 23 November 1993, in a co-production between Boilerhouse and The Lemon Tree. The cast was as follows:

Julie Allardyce	Katrina Caldwell
David Mitchell	Peter Burnett
Finn Finlay	Micky MacPherson
Gary Grant	Andrew Wardlaw
Angela Bruce	Vicki Masson
Drew Allardyce	Steve Webb

Other characters were doubled by the cast and further non-speaking parts were played by: Denise Chapman, Duncan Craig, Linda Davidson, Victoria McLennan, Kim Smith

Directed by Paul Pinson
Designed by Bryan Angus
Lighting Designer Tariq Hussain
Music Ken Slaven

The play is set in the present day, in and around Aberdeen, including some scenes on an offshore drilling rig.

Scene One
Getting there

The audience is sitting in a helicopter, about to fly offshore. The lights go down to black, the engines start up, whining, and gradually build to a deafening roar; there is music in this as well as real industrial noise. Take off. The seats shake and rattle violently. From time to time a distorted radio-voice can be heard saying something indecipherable.

Ahead is a narrow field of vision, sharply lit against the black. Across it bright colours begin to flash: green and yellow, green and yellow, blue and green, blue and green, blue and blue, blue and white, and blue and blue. Then a black appears, a blue and a black and more blues, then another black, then more blacks gradually taking over from the blue till there is only black. The space is filled with dense black – it's impenetrable, but not static: flowing, billowing, rippling – and the movement builds to a climax along with the noise of the helicopter engine.

Then both stop as, for a second, a large white H inside a circle is visible. Touchdown on the platform. Without any let-up, the H is replaced by an enormous roaring red and orange flame overhead. After a few seconds, dozens of small bright lights become visible against the overall darkness: stars and ships and rigs scattered across the sea and sky.

Scene Two
A proposal

Two figures appear and lean against a railing, standing close together, looking out to sea. The flare burns above them, lighting their faces with flickering red and orange. After a few seconds' silence, they speak.

David   Will you marry me?

Julie   Aye, okay then.

Immediately music bursts out, loud and tuneful and joyous: bits of

*the Wedding March and Scottish dance music especially, but also
snatches of a hundred different tunes and moods: all the music
from the rest of the play speeded up and sampled and mixed
together. Again bright colours swirl about, dominated by white and
green around* **Julie**, *blue circling both of them. The cast performs
the whole play in thirty seconds, in abstract, concentrating on the
aspects – and mostly the happy aspects – of* **Julie** *and* **David**
*as a couple. A few seconds from the end, there is a glimpse of red
and black, red and black, before it's back to the white and green
and blue again and the movement and the music stop.* **Julie** *and*
David *stand alone at the railing, the flare burning overhead.*

Julie   But we'll have to keep it quiet.

David   What!

Julie   You ken the rules: no happy couples allowed
offshore.

David   It's not like we're doing it on the drill floor!

Julie   As soon as they spot signs of happiness, we're
back on the beach like a shot.

David   Aye, Grant'd love that: any excuse to cause a
bittie more misery!

Julie   And then what? We'd get alternate shifts, we'd
only meet at Dyce – you coming in just as I was going
out – 'Hi Julie', 'Aye aye Davy' – no way to start a
married life!

David (*looking out over the water*)   Delta looks hell of a
close thenight.

Julie   We'll just have to make on like we're your
average bears with a sore head . . .

David   It looks like you could swim it.

Julie   I'd like to see you try.

He climbs up on the railing, as if about to jump. She laughs.

David   Are you not going to stop me then?

Julie   You'd never do it! You haven't the guts!

David   And you have, like?

Julie   The way I feel just now I could *jump* it, never mind swim it!

She climbs up onto a railing and makes on she's about to leap. He pulls her back laughing.

David   You're mad Julie Allardyce!

Julie   No, just in love.

David   (*the start of a game they play:*)   In love? With who?

Julie   With you!

David   With me?

Julie   With you and me and the whole North Sea! (*She climbs up on the railing again, facing out to the sea, and shouts:*) Julie Allardyce loves you!

She lets herself fall backwards off the railing, and **David** *catches her — it's like a scene from a silent film, them playing the role of the lovers — and they embrace and go to kiss. But somebody walks out towards them:* **Grant**, *going about his business.* **David** *and* **Julie** *split apart and disappear into the shadows before he gets to them. He looks after them — fairly casually, without any melodramatic emphasis — then goes on with his work, which is to shout the line that opens the next scene:*

Grant   Mitchell, get those boxes shifted!

Scene Three
Lowering

Bright daylight. The noise of an oil rig at work. Drills, generators, motors; clanging and hammering; the wind, the sea; shouts, tannoy. A steady green light shines, indicating all is normal.

David *is working loading stores from one place to another. This*

*is repetitive and hard: he lifts a heavy box from one pile, carries it
ten metres, then dumps it in another pile. There are a hundred
boxes to shift.* **Grant***, the deck foreman, is watching him, every
so often directing* **David** *as to exactly which box should be picked
up next and precisely where it should be dumped; he checks his
watch and clipboard often, and keeps* **David** *moving fast.*
Grant *keeps an eye on everything going on around the deck of the
rig, wandering about from time to time to have a closer look at
something. In the foreground, at the edge of the moonpool,* **Julie**
and **Finn** *are doing work that appears more absorbing: pre-dive
checks on the ROV.*

*The noise of the rig at work carries on throughout the scene, almost
like a musical score: sometimes the dialogue is echoed, sometimes
almost drowned out.*

Julie How's the docking dogs?

Finn All three dogs secured.

Julie On the lip?

Finn On the fucking lip.

Julie Docking bullet in place?

Finn Docking bullet fucking home. I'll go and check
the cable.

Julie I already checked the cable.

Finn I'll double fucking check.

Julie Checked?

Finn Check. The cable's fucking coiled.

Julie The drum's wound – I checked.

Finn I fucking know you fucking did, or it wouldn't
been a fucking double fucking check, would it?

Julie A fucking double fucking check?

Finn Fucking right.

Julie   Glad I got something right.

Finn   You're always fucking right, that's why I fucking hate you.

Julie   Get out from inside that bight!

Finn   Jesus fucking Christ! There you go, right again!

Julie   It's not that I don't hate you too . . .

Finn   Right about the bight!

Julie   . . . but I don't want your blood on my machine when you're minced by the cable.

Finn (*stepping out from inside cable*)   Ready to fucking go then.

Julie   I'll tell Control.

Finn   So you're getting the fucking inside job a-fucking-gain?

Julie   You're so good on the winch Finn, that . . .

Finn   Fuck off.

They both work at the winch for a few seconds; the ROV rises up and swings out over the sea. **Julie** *feeds its cable out, making sure it's not twisting etc. When it's in position she leaves the winch and goes into the control shack, sits down in front of the video screens, and picks up the phone there.*

Julie (*she dials the phone*)   ROV module to Rig Control. Aye, that time again. Just to let you ken. All clear to launch? Good. Eh, fifty to a hundred metres depth, corrosion check on the north-west leg. Sure. Aye. Bye. (*Shouting out the door.*) They've given us clear Finn. Ready to go?

Finn   Fucking right I'm fucking ready.

He works at the winch while **Julie** *returns to watch the videos. The screen in front of her is represented by a bright light shining in her face. Over the course of the next few lines all other lighting* *fades away.*

Julie   The raising and lowering, it's the one bit of the job I don't like. I hate it when the ROV's stuck out there in its cage. It's like a dolphin lying on your kitchen table: out of its natural element. But just wait till it gets in the water, then you'll see what it's all about! Dangling about there, swaying and swinging, inching down to the sea – just when I want to get zooming on, on and under the water, aye, that's where me and the ROV should be.

Finn   Okay Julie, ready to drop the fucker.

Julie   This is what it's all about, where you get to grips with the splash zone. (*She puts her hands out to the screen light.*) This is where life gets worth living.

Finn   It's factory work, fuck all else: maintaining and training and checking and trimming: the fact that you're half-way to Norway makes fuck all difference most of the time.

Julie   (*she picks up the screen light. It is a portable lamp with a narrow intense beam. For the moment, it still illuminates her head and hands*)   Union Street looks narrow to the likes of me, it's a single-track back-of-beyond dead-end compared to where I drive. Up and down the North Sea. I drive up and down and east and west and north and south. And I don't drive a Ford or a Datsun or a Beamer. I don't drive a tractor or a bus or a bike. I drive an ROV: remotely operated vehicle.

Finn   (*looking over the edge*)   She's in the fucking water!

The sea has been lying flat beneath them. Now it starts to rise in waves around **Julie** *and* **Finn**. *As the ROV goes through the splash zone, the sea whips up in a frenzy of blue and white.*

Julie   And we're through the swell and the waves: welcome to my world. (*She stands up, moving the lamp so its beam is shining out in front of her.*) Five metres, ten, fifteen.

Down a bit more then I'll let off the clamps, release the rams – eighteen, nineteen, twenty – and *out* we go, out of the cage into freedom, freedom! (*She leaves her seat and wanders around inside the sea, the light beaming out through the waves.*) Where the water's over deep for divers, the ROV goes twice as deep. And in my head, and on the screens, I go scouting with it. Headlights on in the dark black depths, and I see things that no one's seen, the floor of the sea, the rocks and the sand, the fish and the weed and the reefs and the wrecks. I've eyes as sharp as a shark's, see landshifts under pipelines or cracks in concrete platforms through water dark as squid ink. In control, in front of the monitors, the joystick and the instrument panels; I'm the one in the driving seat.

The blue of the sea begins to be replaced by black. By the end of **Julie***'s lines, she is completely surrounded by swirling dark waters. Likewise, faint noises of the sea – gurgling water, winds, foghorns and hooters, sonar beeps – fade in, get louder and louder, till by the end of the speech they are almost drowning her out. Through it all she works with great concentration.*

Julie   Half a ton, six feet long, half a million quid! One thousand miles by five hundred miles by three thousand metres of the world's coldest, blackest, stormiest water and it's mine to wander in! Julie Allardyce, twenty-two, eighteen grand a year! To boldly go where no Julie's gone before: down and down and down and down and down and down and down . . .

The black swirls viciously around **Julie***, hiding her completely: blackout.*

Scene Four
In dreams

The sea noises mix with and gradually change into general storm noises: waves crashing, wind howling, the rig creaking. Lights up inside the smoko shack, where the deck workers are sheltering.

Grant *paces up and down.* **Julie** *stares into space.* **David** *and* **Finn** *play cards.*

Grant Jesus Christ, this weather!

Nobody responds.

Grant Do you know how much this is costing us?

Finn It's not costing me anything.

Grant It's costing the company though – fucking millions! – and anything that costs the company costs us all in the long run.

Finn Bollocks.

Grant (*looks out a window*) I reckon the wind's dropping a bit lads.

An enormous gust of wind shakes the shack, and water smashes against the window.

David If you ever leave the oil, Mr Grant, don't go for a job as a weather forecaster.

Grant See in Saudi? You don't get weather like this out there!

Finn Aye, and you don't get a fucking drink either, so fuck that for a game of soldiers.

Grant Anybody has a drink out *here* is fucked, and don't you forget it, Finlay. (*Glances at* **Julie**.) And another thing that should be banned: women. No more women working offshore!

David There's only about twenty as it is, for fuck's sake.

Grant Ah, that's the way it used to be, when we still had our heads screwed on. But nowadays they're popping up left right and centre.

Finn I wish one would pop up in my bunk.

Grant Exactly: they come offshore and they start stirring things up. We're meant to be doing a job of work out here, but you start bringing women into it and straight away men's minds get distracted – am I not right Mitchell? – and before you know it there's ill discipline and mistakes being made and rows breaking out: some men just can't handle having women close by, eh Mitchell?

David *looks completely blank.*

Grant Before you know it the whole rig's just in an uproar.

Finn *and* **David** *look at each other, then over at* **Julie**, *who is sitting still, in silence, apparently not hearing at all what the others are saying.*

Finn Hey, Julie.

Julie Eh?

David Cheer up Julie.

Finn Julie's always fucking cheerful.

Julie Aye, I am, but I just . . . had something nagging at me.

David Aye, it was Mr Grant . . .

Finn Do you hear the uproar you're causing out here. It's a fucking disgrace girl! The whole North Sea's whipped up into a frenzy of ill discipline and rows cause of you!

Julie What shite are you talking now, Finn?

Finn It's not me Julie, it's Mr Ops Controller here, he was giving us a wee educational lecture while rain stopped play. Is that not right Mr Grant?

Grant Another thing is, can you tell me, has it ever been *scientifically proved* that women can do the job as well as men?

David Has it been proved that they can't?

Grant Ah, but innocent till proved guilty Mitchell! Men have been innocently going about their lives for thousands of years – taking the *man*'s share of the hard work – and all of a sudden women start saying that they can work just as hard. Well, fuck me with a drill pipe, could they not just've left things the way they were? Mark my words, the day'll soon come when women are banned to the beach.

Finn In your dreams, Grant . . .

Julie (*claps her hands, turns to* **Finn**, *suddenly full of energy*) That's it Finn, a dream! It was a dream!

Finn What?

Julie I had these pictures going through my head, but I couldn't understand them. It was nagging at me: was that a film I saw? did it happen to me sometime? was it a story I read? But no, now I ken, it was a dream! And I never dream! Usually I just come straight awake as soon as the alarm goes, ken, awake and straight into the business of the day. I haven't bothered with dreams for years. But last night I had one. It was so real! Christ, it's hard to believe that's all it was. I really thought I was out on the deck there, at the side of the moonpool.

David Well, you were out there yesterday.

Julie Aye, but this was different, cause yesterday Finn was working with me. In my dream I was all alone, just me and the ROV. It wasn't behaving just right, so I'd opened a front pod and had my hand inside it, working away, checking the circuit boards. Then suddenly something gripped my hand. Inside the pod something had a hold of my fingers and was trying to pull them in. I snatch my hand away, but it comes just an inch then gets gripped again, and now something sharp's biting my skin. My skin's tearing, more the more I pull away, and under the skin the bones are being squeezed till they crush. I bang my free hand on the side of the ROV and yell with the pain. But no one's around to help me: the deck's empty of folk.

Grant   Where were you Finlay? You should've been there as well.

Julie   But there *was* a voice, a voice murmuring something . . . I looked around, my hand tearing and crushing inside the pod as I jerked this way and that. No one in sight, but still the voice.

ROV (*a voice over the tannoy*)   Feed me, I'm hungry, feed me.

Julie   My hand's being mangled. I try to scream out, but the voice speaks again.

ROV   Feed me, I'm hungry, feed me.

Julie   I stare at the ROV. 'Let me go,' I say. 'You can't eat me.' And for a second there's silence, and I think, My God, I'm going mad, talking to a machine! Then the voice comes again.

ROV   Feed me, I'm hungry, feed me.

Julie   'You can't eat me, you'd be lost without me, wouldn't know where to go, wouldn't know how to get there. You can't eat me, let me go!'

ROV   But I'm hungry, you wouldn't let me starve would you? You're supposed to look after me, but now you're letting me starve! Feed me!

Julie   And its teeth close tighter on my flesh and bone. 'You can't eat me now, I'm getting married theday.' Cause suddenly I mind I'm meant to be at the kirk, at my wedding, not out on the rig; already I'm hell of a late. 'Let me go thenow, and I'll come back later and feed you.'

ROV   I'll be *really* hungry by then. (*It laughs.*) But okay Julie, it's a deal, come back later and feed me well and

I'll let you go just now.

Julie   'Thanks,' I say, and go to pull my hand out, but just as I do there's a stabbing pain, and a grinding noise, a tearing, riving agony, and my hand comes away, gouting with blood, and the ROV's making clanking chewing noises and laughing away to itself. I lift my hand up before my eyes, and then I scream out loud. 'The wedding's off! Call off the marriage! I'll never get married now!'

ROV   Why's that, Julie?

Julie   And I stare at my hand, my left hand, the hand with one finger eaten away, the third finger on my left hand, ripped off inside the ROV's mouth. Nowhere to put the ring!

Julie *ends up with her supposedly mutilated hand held up in front of her. She stares at it in horror. The story has been told so convincingly that everyone else is staring at her hand too. After a couple of seconds,* **Finn** *breaks the tension.*

Finn   Do you want an elastoplast for that?

David   Jesus, what a nightmare.

Grant   Hold on a minute, what's all this about a wedding?

Julie   I'm *glad* I don't usually dream! Better off without them!

Grant   No, just cause any change of circumstances should be reported to the company, and I don't recall reading that you were getting married.

David   What?

Grant   And who are you getting married to Julie? Anybody we know? I mean this could be important.

Julie   Eh, Mr Grant . . . it was a dream.

Grant   Is that all? No plans even?

Julie Who do you think I am? Nostrajulius, predicting the future in my sleep?

David Aye, good question though Julie: what the fuck does it *mean*, eh?

Finn It means she's been reading too much Stephen fucking King again.

Grant See what I mean lads? Women: they're off in a fucking dream world! And we trust her with company ROVs that cost millions of quid! The whole production relies on her sometimes, and she's away in a dream world!

Julie I was asleep in my cabin at the time.

Finn (*laughs*) Ach, excuses!

Grant (*looks outside*) The weather's definitely turning: on deck, you work-shy cunts.

The others groan, but follow him out as he opens the door of the shack. Immediately they are battered by a raging gale, and torrents of blue and black water wash around and above them, swallowing them completely. Mixed in with the wind and water noises is a foghorn, blasting away: short short long, short short long.

Scene Five
From The Crow's Nest

A brightly lit stair. **Julie** *is standing at the door of her friend* **Angela**'s *flat in one of the Seaton blocks. She reaches out and presses the doorbell, a foghorn sounds. The door opens.*

Angela Julie!

Julie That's a hell of a funny doorbell you've got!

Angela Mental, eh? The old guy that lived here afore me was a sailor, ken?

Julie Well, he got a good view of the sea, I suppose.

Angela   God aye. If you go out on the balcony on a windy night you get spray off the beach on your face.

Julie   Nah!

Angela   Aye!

Julie   Thirteen floors up?

Angela   Aye! The old guy had a nameplate on the door, 'The Crow's Nest', but I took it down. Didn't want anybody calling me an old bird!

Julie   So, Angela, can I come in? Or do you entertain your pals on the doormat these days?

Angela   No, no, come in. But shh! Quiet in the lobby, or you'll wake him up.

Julie (*pausing on the point of entering*)   Wake who?

Angela   Derek! Who else?

Julie   For a second I thought you'd maybe taken Crazy Colin back.

Angela   No chance. He doesn't even ken where I'm living these days, and he's not going to find out.

Julie   What do you tell Derek?

Angela   He asked me once where his daddy was, and I says he was dead. Well, I said he was in heaven.

Julie   Colin Birse in heaven? That's a good one!

Angela   Stranger things've happened ... maybe.

Julie   Aye, they have, and I've got one to tell you thenow.

They go into the living-room of **Angela**'s *flat.* **Julie** *sits on the settee, looks around;* **Angela** *clears up toys and books from the floor, slings them into a box.*

Julie   So, settling in okay are you?

Angela Settling in? I've been here near a year!

Julie Christ, is it that long?

Angela Aye, it's that long.

Julie Well, I . . . hey, *you* could've given *me* a ring too!

Angela Ach, you and your high-flying lifestyle . . . I thought you'd given up on the likes of me: work-shy doley scroungers.

Julie Don't be daft. I've just, I don't ken, I never seem to have time and . . . I did send you a Christmas card.

Angela Oh aye, and thanks for Derek's presents: he loved that book where you pressed the buttons and it made the noise of a helicopter and a fire engine and that.

Julie Did you tell him I was coming?

Angela No. He'd just've wanted to bide up and see you, he'd've been up for hours. Me and you'd never've got a chance to talk.

Julie Do you think he'd mind who I was?

Angela Oh definitely: his Aunty Julie. Something reminds him whiles, and he asks after you.

Julie Aunty Julie!

Angela It's funny, he doesn't call his real aunties Aunty, he just calls them by their names. It's only you gets the honour of Aunty.

Julie Maybe cause they're younger, like.

Angela Maybe.

Julie Though I suppose they're . . .

Angela Carrie's fifteen and Lauren's sixteen.

Julie Is that right? Still, that is hell of a young.

Angela Just kids.

Julie You couldn't've told me that when I was sixteen. 'Just a kid!'

Angela Ha! You thought you were the last word.

Julie What? So did you!

Angela Aye, but I *was* the last word, that's the difference.

Both laugh.

Julie Aye, you were a bad lot Angie-baby. A glue sniffer. My daddy told me about folk like you.

Angela Mind that time I got you to spray that graffiti outside the science block: 'Sandra Tait is a blowjob!'

Julie Hih. I never even kent what a blowjob was!

Angela Did you not?

Julie I thought it was something to do with hairdressing.

Both laugh.

Angela Here, Julie.

Julie What?

Angela What *is* a blowjob?

Both laugh.

Julie If you don't ken by now . . .

Both . . . you never will.

Angela Aye, but think about it, eh Julie? What if we had known then what we know now?

Julie This is it, I did know then! Like when we were about ten and we all hated loons, just couldn't stand them, and everybody was saying how they were never going to get married and that. I mind you saying you'd never have nothing to do with men as long as you lived!

Angela   I should've listened to myself, eh?

Julie   But all the time folk were saying this, and I was kind of going along with it, I was really thinking, no, everybody does get married and I'm not going to be left out; I don't ken *why* they get married, but whatever it is changes and makes them, well, that'll happen to me as well I bet! I kent then that that would happen to me. And now it has: I'm getting married.

Angela   You were so *logical* about everything, Julie! Such a *sensible* bitch! But . . . hold on! What did you just say?

Julie   Eh . . . aye. That's what I was wanting to tell you.

Angela   Wooo! So who is the lucky bugger?

Julie   What do you mean who is it – it's David of course! Do you think I'd go out with him for two and a half year, then marry some other body all of a sudden? Terrible waste of effort!

Angela   What does your brother think?

Drew *wanders across the stage singing the start of the classic Strathdon ballad, 'Drumallochie'.* **Angela** *and* **Julie** *don't see him. The feeling should be quite ghostly; there could be a fiddle playing softly behind him.*

Drew
  'Twas on a chill November's night when fruits and
    flowers were gone
  One evening as I wandered forth upon the banks of
    Don
  I overheard a fair maid and sweetly thus sang she
  'My love he's far from Sinnahard and from
    Drumallochie'

Drew *whistles or hums a few more bars as he wanders off, then* *back to the women as if nothing has happened.*

Julie (*surprised at her question*) Drew? Who cares! Damn all to do with him! Why?

Angela *avoids answering the question by getting up and wandering out the glass door at the end of the room.*

Julie Where are you going?

Angela It's a fine night, I fancied a seat on the balcony.

Julie (*following her*) There's no seats out here . . .

Angela Not *in* the balcony, *on* it.

The two of them sit on the ledge. **Angela** *is calm, gazes out over the lights of the city, but* **Julie** *peers anxiously down for a while, before speaking again.*

Julie We're going to see David's ma and da the morn. Tell them the good news.

Angela How do you get on with them?

Julie Better than you get on with yours.

Angela Well, that's not saying much.

Julie (*thinks*) They must like to see Derek though?

Angela Oh aye, they're all over him! They forget all the weeks they spent persuading me to kill him.

Julie What?

Angela To have an abortion.

Julie (*pause*) Aye, they did, didn't they. Still, it's a while ago now.

Angela Aye. (*Pause.*) He starts school next year.

Julie You're joking.

Angela No, really.

Julie Jesus Christ.

Angela No, it's good though.

Julie Aye, it's just . . .

Angela I'll have a lot more time, ken.

Julie Aye, it's good. It's just – starting school! – Christ, *we* were at school just the other day!

Angela Then I'm going to try and get into the college, get some highers. Second time lucky!

Julie It's unbelievable that you could leave school, have a kid, and before you know it your *own* kid's starting school!

Angela Course I'd've saved myself a lot of trouble if I'd got them five year ago.

Julie Ho! Too right! You spent more time slagging me off for being a swot than you did doing any work!

Angela Course, would I be any better off? I mean if I'd got highers and a job and got married and all that, I'd probably be just *starting* to think about having a kid now. Instead here I am, four years ahead of the game!

Julie That's one way of looking at it I suppose.

Angela Aye, my way. There's times I feel like jumping off that balcony, but on the whole I'm really happy the way it's ended up. But then I'd nothing to lose – except Colin. And a lot of bruises. Aye, losing him turned out to be the best thing I ever did. That's the difference atween me and you: you've a lot to lose.

Julie Aye I have: I've everything! My job. My car. My flat. Aye that's another thing: we were kids just the other day, and now I look round and I've all this stuff, adult stuff attached to me! It's scary sometimes.

Angela The more you have, the more you have to lose, eh?

Julie I had to fight to get my training, then to get my job, and now I'm fighting to keep it! Well, I'm keeping my mouth shut to keep it.

Angela Christ, that must be a struggle for you!

Julie You're not allowed to be a couple offshore, you see. We had a few fights over it, like, but I think he's seen sense now: after we're married David'll hand in his notice and ... try and find work on the beach.

Angela What, like deckchair attendant?

Julie Eh? Oh! No!

Laughter. **Angela** *jumps up again.*

Julie Where are you going now?

Angela The view's so good here, I bet it's even better from the top.

Julie (*going after her*) The top of what?

Angela (*running upstairs now*) The roof! Come on!

The two of them run up many flights of stairs and onto the flat roof of the block. They go and sit on the edge, legs dangling into twenty floors of space, looking out at the sea.

Angela So. You must be really happy, Julie.

Julie What do you mean?

Angela I was just thinking: you must be really *happy*.

Julie Like I say, I've got everything I ever wanted.

Angela Aye. (*Looking at* **Julie**, *doubtful for a moment.*) But ... are you happy?

Julie I don't know what you're getting at.

Angela Well, I haven't got anything that I wanted – I never got to art school, never went out on the ran-dan with Shane MacGowan, never got to travel round the world like I wanted to – but I'm happy. Things've turned out exactly the way I *didn't* want them, but I'm happy. You're the opposite of me, Julie, you've got everything you wanted when you were sixteen – qualifications, money, a good job, your own flat in the middle of town, a good man that's marrying you – everything!

Julie   Aye, there you go: your question's answered.

Angela   But it's not.

Julie   Eh?

Angela   You've got it all, but are you happy with it?

Julie   I never thought about it like that, I never stopped to think about it at all really. I just ... I just took it for granted. But *am* I happy? Christ, I've no idea!

Angela   I mean I'm not saying you're not ...

Julie   I ken.

Angela   I was just asking cause I haven't seen you for ages and I wondered ...

Julie   Aye.

Angela   I mean you probably are.

Julie   Aye. Probably. I'll have to think about it.

Angela (*after a second's silence to let* **Julie** *think*)   So what's your life going to be like once you're married then?

Julie   I don't know. The same as just now, I suppose, except I'll have a ring on my finger. And we'll spend every night thegether instead of just most nights.

Angela   When you get married Julie ... you're not just marrying a man, you're marrying a whole life.

Julie   Nah, not me: I've already got a life.

Angela   It's like having a baby. You're not just giving birth to a wee greeting and shitting machine, you're giving birth to your *own life* for the next . . . five years . . . twenty years! They don't tell you that, but that's what you find out: the baby changes your whole life. I mean I ken you must've thought about it, you must be pretty sure that this is the man you want, this is the *life* you want, but . . . I just thought I'd mention it.

Julie Aye. Thanks. (*Pause.*) Christ, it's a long way down, isn't it?

Scene Six
Bonnie Ythanside

Drew *yanks at* **Julie**'s *arm and pulls her off the balcony ledge and into an argument. They are on the Allardyce farm, Ythanbanks, near Woodhead of Fyvie. The argument starts off being a friendly one, with their fighting being an affectionate brother / sister thing, but after a while there does seem to be real anger bubbling just under the surface, coming out into the open, even.*

Drew What are you like, Julie, coming out here and telling me you're getting married? What are you like for fuck's sake?

Julie Like a sister, I suppose.

Drew Damn the bit.

Julie I don't ken why you're so put out by me getting married . . .

Drew I'm not!

Julie . . . unless it's cause you've never managed it.

Drew Listen, you peenge, there's women queuing up to be the wife on this farm!

Julie Aye, the farm's a good catch. Just a shame you come along with it.

Drew   Oh aye, it's all coming out now!

Julie   What?

Drew   You're out here after the farm! 'A good catch' is it? My arse!

Julie   What are you talking about Drew?

Drew   This was decided years ago: two hundred acre, there's only a living for one of us here, and it makes sense for it to be me.

Julie   (*pause*)   I ken that was decided.

Drew   I tell you, the living here is a thin one: no way could it support the both of us – let alone ... somebody else as well.

Julie   I've got a job, so has David.

Drew   Well keep a hold of them, cause I've got the farm.

Julie   I'm not needing to work here.

Drew   Too much work for not enough pay, eh?

Julie   I just don't fancy it.

Drew   You've gone awful sappy, quine. That oil's made you soft, I reckon.

Julie   Shows how little you ken about working offshore.

Drew   I ken this: you don't impress me Julie.

Julie   Do you think that's why I do it?

Drew   Maybe.

Julie *takes a swing at* **Drew**. *He dodges it. She tries to hit him again, and this time he has to parry the blow. They circle around, each trying to get a grip or land a blow on the other, till after a few seconds they make a lunge for each other, miss, and* **Drew** *disappears.* **Julie** *is immediately in conversation with* **David**, *as if nothing had happened.*

David Tell me about it then. I can see it gets to you.

Julie Eh?

David You're always so happy on the way out here, but as soon as we arrive you start getting edgy.

Julie Edgy?

David Aye. What is it – Drew? You always seem to be getting at each other.

Julie That's just kidding though; there's nothing in it.

David Is there not?

Julie Me and Drew ... we always mess around like that. We get on fine though, always have. When we were kids, right, we had these bunk beds – him up on top, me down below – and it was a brilliant laugh. We'd tell each other stories half the night, things we'd heard on the school bus, or from my granny and granda in Fyvie. We'd just take bits of their stories and add our own bits on when we couldn't remember something. It was great.

David I always wished I had a brother for stuff like that. Or a sister even. Christ, even a dog would've been something! But we lived in this wee flat so ...

Julie I mind we used to pretend the bunk beds were a ship. We'd hang blankets over the sides and there I'd be working away down in the boiler rooms of the bottom bunk, shovelling coal into the furnaces behind the pillow. And Drew'd be up top, on the bridge, with the compass and the tea tray for a steering wheel. (*Pause.*) I always wanted to be the one up top, steering the ship, but I never got to be. Only boys got to do that. Quines had to stay down in the galleys: galley slaves!

David Where would you have steered for if you'd been captain?

Julie Ach, I don't ken. Nowhere. It was just wanting

to be steering was the important bit, not where I was
going.

Out of nowhere, **Drew** *jumps on top of* **Julie***, and they fight
again, more seriously this time. They roll around in front of*
David*, but he doesn't see them. Then the fight suddenly stops
again.*

David   I always wished I could have a brother or a
sister, just for things like that. I missed all that stuff.

Julie   You always got on well with your folks though.

David   Well, I had to, in a way, I mean it was just me
and them in the house. Usually I couldn't bring my pals
from school home even, cause my dad was on nights at
the printers', and he was asleep all through the day
when I wanted to be playing. The main thing when I
was a kid was keeping quiet.

Julie   Not much wonder you grew up weird!

David   Strong but silent, you mean?

Julie   Aye, weird.

David   And by the time my dad left the printers' I was
already started offshore, so ... (*He shrugs.*) To be honest
I'm glad I was, cause I reckon he was even worse for a
while after that.

Julie   Till you got him the job with security.

David   For a year or so he was a nightmare, my mum
said. And he'd have to be really bad afore she'd
complain.

Julie   It's amazing what folk put up with, out of habit
just.

Julie *sees* **Drew** *coming, and jumps up to meet the attack. After
a few blows, they reach a stalemate, their hands around each
other's throat, and they argue instead:*

Julie   You always hated me working offshore, cause I

earned more siller than you. You can't stand that, a woman showing you up.

Drew Nobody's showing me up. I do good honest work here.

Julie And the work me and David do isn't honest, is that what you're saying?

Drew Maybe.

Julie I'll tell you, Andrew, you don't ken what work is! Honest or dishonest, it's work I've been doing, work that puts pounds in the bank. All you've earned is subsidies, EurofuckingDisney money!

Drew Come on, out with it.

Julie With what?

Drew With what you really want to say. Come on you bastard, say it.

Back to the quiet chat, though **Julie** *is clearly getting more worked up now:*

David Okay, you used to get on so well with him, but when did you fall out?

Julie We never did! We get on fine.

David Julie, anybody can see you just rub each other up the wrong way. What went wrong?

Julie Nothing went wrong! (*Pause.*) It's just, I suppose, things did start to change atween us around the time that, well, when they found the first tumour in my dad's gut. I was twelve, Drew was about fourteen. From then on he changed, he didn't want anything to do with me after that. He just started hanging around my dad all the time, not even speaking to me.

David I suppose that's natural, really. I mean if he thought your dad was away to, eh, to die, maybe, I suppose he would've wanted to spend time with him.

Julie   It was three and a half years afore he died.

David   But nobody could've known how long . . .

Julie   It wasn't that Drew wanted to spend time with him, just for the being with him. It was like Drew started copying him, trying to turn into him. Wearing his old bunnets at the age of fourteen for God's sake!

David   I suppose he kent then – sooner than he wanted, maybe – that he'd have to take over the running of Ythanbanks.

Julie (*furious*)   Aye, that's what *he* decided. *He* decided then that *he* would take over, that he would farm the place when dad died. And how about me? He decided I wouldn't get a look in! He decided it was going to be his, he'd have it all himself, there was no place for me there. He decided I'd have to bugger off away from our land and work at something else, only come back for an afternoon once a month and even then not be allowed to have a say in the running of the place. And why? Cause I was handless? Cause I didn't ken about farming? No! Just cause I was a quine and he was a loon, that was all it was, that's what disqualified me from working on the land.

David (*he is shocked; this is the first time there's been such an outburst of bad feeling from* **Julie**)   Julie, calm down.

Julie   Calm down? He decided all this when I was bloody twelve. And I never got to say a word about it. That was it. Twelve. Finished. Chucked off the land. Chucked off my own land.

Drew *appears again, and* **Julie** *leaps up to face him. They are both tense, ready to fight, but instead are shouting:*

Drew   Come on, say it.

Julie   No.

Drew   Out with it.

Julie No, I don't want to.

Drew Come on, you bastard.

Julie (*with a new ferocity*) Okay, I want it, I want this land, this is *my* land, not just yours, it belonged to my father and mother, and to my father's mother and father afore, and it's not something that can be taken away from me – even by you. It's inside me. This earth, me, I want it, I need it. See? See, you bugger? It's inside me. It is me. I belong here, this is my home, let me back – let me work here!

Drew (*pause*) Farming's changed, Julie. It's always changing, I ken that, but this past few year it's been quick change, ken? Hard to keep up with. And they're not changes for the better. (*He looks around.*) There's not work for you here. There's nothing for you here.

Julie There is work. Look around! I can see it!

Drew There is work, but there's no money. There's not a living on this land for you any more.

Julie Aye but, no, no . . . look, I told you already, I don't want to work here, I've got a good job, I like my job, the pay's great and . . .

Drew Will you make up your mind then? First you want to come here, then you don't; you swan it over me for years cause you're working in the oil, and now you're turning round and saying . . .

Julie I don't ken what I want. I want Ythanbanks. I know this place so I want to be here, I want to be somewhere I know.

Drew You don't ken this place any more, Julie. You left, and you can't come back.

Julie But I have come back, I'm here!

Drew See that river down there quine? It's still the Ythan, same as when we were bairns; doesn't mean it's the same water flowing by that we used to guddle in.

Julie (*after a pause for thought*) Mind, we used to aye be piling up boulders and bits of wood and that, trying to build dams across the river.

Drew They never worked though.

Julie They aye got washed away.

Drew It's a fact quine. You've got to face up to facts.

Scene Seven
Facts are chiels that winna ding

From various parts of the stage, and all around the theatre, the rest of the cast troop on. Their arrival is preceded by a tremendously loud rattling and banging, for they are carrying or wearing various oil drums, canisters, and petrol tins, which they beat with drumsticks. They also drum on objects and surfaces all around the stage. Out of the racket emerges a regular rhythm, and under the rhythm a chanting begins to be heard:

Drummers Face the facts, face the facts, face the facts, face the facts . . .

*The drummers form a circle around the stage, and their speed and loudness increase. Suddenly there is a very brief pause, long enough for **Julie** to shout:*

Julie Whose facts?

Five seconds' more drumming, then another brief pause:

Drew Facts are facts!

*The drummers restart immediately, and from their positions marking time at the edge of the stage start to spiral in, getting closer and closer to **Julie** and **Drew** standing in the middle of the stage. Their chant has changed:*

Drummers Facts are chiels that winna ding, facts are chiels that winna ding . . .

The drummers are in a close circle around **Drew** *and* **Julie**, *drumming right in their faces. After a few seconds of this,* **Julie** *leaps forward and breaks through the circle.*

Julie Show me!

The drummers immediately stop drumming and start shouting out the following facts and figures, competing with each other to get them over to **Julie** *and to the audience. Divide the lines up between individuals and groups as appropriate. The whole lot should be put over quickly – in about thirty seconds – with much overlapping, and often conflicting messages being given simultaneously. It's the overall battery of information that's important, not the successful transmission of any one 'fact'.*

Drummers Farming's been our heartblood for five thousand years.
Farming earns four hundred million pounds a year for the North-East.
Five thousand years!
That's a tenth of all our income.
Oil's been around for twenty.
The number of hired farm workers has fallen by more than a third over the last twenty years.
There's a record number of farmers going bust.
More farmers kill themselves than any other profession.
Over sixty per cent of the cattle slaughtered in the region are born elsewhere.
The government pay farmers not to grow crops: they call it set-aside, I call it lunacy.
Consumption of beef's at a hundred-year low.
Production of oil seed rape's at an all-time high.
Farms are getting bigger.
Farms are getting fewer.
The small farms are being swallowed up.
The small farmers're getting squeezed out.
Farms are turning over faster than ever before.
Farmers from outside the area are taking over more than ever before.
Farming's the heartblood of the North-East.

Has been for thousands of years.
Will be for thousands more.
Oil's been around for twenty.
Oil's about to run out.

Julie Stop.

The drummers freeze.

Julie Half of these facts is wrong! 'Oil's been around
for twenty'? Oil's been here for three hundred million
years!

Drew But you know what they mean.

Julie Aye, but that's not the facts, that's just opinions.
Come on, let's hear the other side of the story.

*The drummers start shouting out again, oil facts this time. Possibly
some of them could be communicated by other means – e.g. slides,
sandwich-boards, banners, back-projection, passing notes amongst
the audience – as well as shouting.*

Drummers Oil is three hundred million years old.
It's the power that drives the whole world.
It's keeping the whole British economy afloat.
Oil is a bituminous liquid resulting from the
decomposition of marine or land plants, and perhaps
also of some non-nitrogenous animal tissues.
Oil is money.
Actually, North Sea oil is only about one hundred and
forty million years old, i.e. it was largely formed during
the Jurassic Period. Funnily enough, Steven Spielberg
has yet to make a film about it, perhaps because
decomposing vegetable matter would be hard to market
as a cuddly toy or a lunch-box.
Oil is Scotland's ticket to prosperous independence.
Oil is the only reason Scotland hasn't been allowed to
break away.
Oil is going to come out of the North Sea for at least
sixty more years.
Oil is going to finish in sixty years and then we'll get

our independence.

Eh . . .

Oil is god.

Oil is power.

Oil is the devil.

Oil is the biggest of the world's big industries.

Oil is measured in barrels of exactly forty-two gallons;
the figure was established in 1482 by King Edward IV
of England as the standard size for transporting and
trading in herring, at that time the most valuable
commodity exported from the North Sea.

Oil is all around this town, like the flood all around the
ark of Noah; after the black flood ebbs, will Aberdeen
be left high and dry?

Oil is used to light the fuels of hell; I beg all concerned
to cease further drilling forthwith, lest the flames of
Satan's realm should be quenched for lack of fuel, and
the sinners of the centuries escape their rightful torture.

Oil is a non-renewable energy resource.

Oil is the preserved urine of whales.

Oil is the blood of the living planet, the seas its
perspiration, the grass and trees its hair, the hills pimples
on the face of the earth.

Oil is John D. Rockefeller.

Oil is Armand Hammer.

Oil is Samuel Samuels, Henri Deterding, John Paul
Getty, Calouste Gulbenkian, Josef Stalin, Saddam
Hussein, Buckskin Joe, Red Adair, Ronnie
MacDonald . . .

Oil is me.

Oil is you.

*By this time the shouting should have been orchestrated into a peak
of noise and quite likely confusion. (It doesn't matter if there's
confusion, in fact it's desirable.) At its peak, the noise is cut clean
off, and **Julie** speaks.*

Julie   I wish I'd never asked now.

Drummers   Facts!

Julie That wasn't any help, it just confused things more!

Drummers Face the facts!

Julie You made it seem like oil and farming were opposites, were enemies, like it was a competition between the two of them!

Drummers Facts!

Julie But that's not right, it's simplistic, it's a distortion: it makes the facts into lies!

Drummers Face the facts!

Julie Forget the facts! What about real life?

Instant blackout and instant launch into the – totally contrasting – next scene.

Scene Eight
Happy families

The Mitchell family living-room. Very cosy. It is some time after the news of the proposal has been broken, and cheery chat continues. **David***'s mother* **Barbara** *leads the conversation, with* **Julie***'s backing, and despite disruption from* **David** *and his father* **John***, who has his own say direct to the audience.*

Barbara (*getting up from the tea-table*) I suppose I better do the dishes then.

Julie Sit down Mrs Mitchell. Me and David'll do them in a minute.

David (*mutters*) Speak for yourself.

John You'll have to watch this one, son!

David That's okay, I like watching her.

Julie You're so romantic, dear.

John   Takes after his old man.

Barbara   Ha, you're joking! (*To* **Julie**.) Did I ever tell you how *we* got married?

David   At the point of a shotgun, was it not?

John   Oi!

Barbara   No, I mean how your father proposed to me.

John *and* **David**   Not that old story!

Julie   What is it? Is it a good one?

Barbara   Well . . .

John   She's lying.

Barbara   I haven't told her yet! How do you ken I was going to lie?

John   Your lips were moving.

David   Dear oh dear!

Barbara   I will ignore his insults, as always. He wasn't always so bold, you see Julie.

David   Was he not?

Barbara   No, he was right quiet! See when he first came up from down south? He never opened his mouth.

David   And now you don't get the chance, eh!

Julie   Wheesht!

John   (*direct to audience. This speech, and* **John**'s *other direct addresses, should overlap with the other characters' speeches following them*)   I wouldn't say I resent it. That's too strong. I mean it does piss me off a bittie – excuse my language – or at least it did, aye it did piss me off. But not now. Now I'm over it. I'm grateful to him. Hih, of course I am. (*Pause.*) But still it doesn't seem quite right

to me, my own laddie having to provide me with a job.
Ken?

Barbara   We started going out when we were real
young, you see Julie, younger than you even, I was just
out of the school in fact, and we kept company for, oh,
years; I mean things did move slower in those days if
you know what I mean . . .

David   I thought this was the swinging sixties?

John   The sixties didn't begin till 1975 in Aberdeen,
son, and even then they weren't very swinging.

Barbara   . . . but even by those standards he was a
slow mover. All the way through his apprenticeship we
went out.

Julie   At the printers'?

John   Aye, any time she'd gone in a huff and wouldn't
let me touch her, she'd say she was feart of me leaving
big inky-black handprints on her dress for the
neighbours to see. Call me a slow mover!

Barbara   You and your pawing!

David   Ma, you'll make me puke!

Julie (*frowning at* **David** *to shut up*)   So what happened
next?

Barbara   Well, we were out walking about the Duthie
Park one night, and we'd been all through the winter
gardens and never a word from him. All those cactuses
made his mouth dry, he said.

John (*direct to audience again*)   I mean it should really be
the other way round, ken? That's how you picture it.
Providing for your kid, bringing them up, getting them
through school. And then, when they leave, you maybe
have a word in the ear of somebody at your work, get
the boy a start. But: twenty-four year in that printshop,
and then one night I find I'm not printing the morning
paper, I'm printing redundancy notices, and one of

them's mine! So I couldn't get him a start; he had to get me one!

Barbara It was a fine summer's night, the flowers were all out in the park and the stars in the sky, and there were couples sitting about on the grass kissing. And somebody had a radio with them and as we passed it was playing a love song. And I turned to him and I said, John, we've been going out thegether a fair long time now. Ihm-hm, he says. Five years I make it. That's me. Here's him: Five years? Ihm-hm. Well John, I said, Do you not think it's about time we was getting married? (*Pause.*) Ihm-hm, he says, and then he walks on. I follow after him, but for ten minutes he doesn't speak a word. I grab his arm, Here, Johnny, I said, You're not saying much for somebody that's just . . . proposed marriage. No Barbara, he says, That's just it: I've said over much already!

Laughter.

John Aye, and maybe I had.

Julie So that is how it happened then?

John No! There's not a word of truth in the whole damn . . . Ach, that's it, I'm away out. Come on David, I'll buy you a dram (*Turning to audience.*) So I wouldn't say I resent David getting me the job. I mean it was me who got myself the job, really. Okay, he fixed up the interview and that, cause the company like different folk in a family working for it. But it was me who actually did the bloody interview. Not that they asked much. I mean, security guard, what are they going to ask you? Ever pocketed any major oil installations? No? You're in! (*Pause.*) It wouldn't've been like that a few years ago, that's all I'm saying. New technology put me out of a job, and it's the new technology that David works with. Of course he got me a job. It's the way the world is these days: totally buggered.

Barbara   See this Julie? It's started already.

David   Mother, shut your face.

Julie   I could come too.

David   I thought you were volunteering to do the dishes?

Julie   Aye, but if you help as well they'll be done in no time and I could . . . aye, and your mum too . . . we could all go out for a drink.

John   Come on *David*, the whisky's evaporating while we speak. (*To audience.*) Twenty year ago it wouldn't've happened, that's all I'm saying. The whole town's been turned upside down, and a lot of folk like me with it. (*As he leaves, ignoring his wife.*) You have to hold on to what you can.

David (*shrugs in what is meant to be an apology*)   See you later.

Julie   See you.

She goes to kiss him, despite obviously being pissed off; he tries to avoid her, but she gets him.

Barbara   Hoi, you're not married yet.

John   That's well seen.

Laughter.

The two men come forwards, out of the house. They are still laughing. Then **John** *stops, and grabs* **David** *by the elbow. Simultaneously,* **Barbara** *grabs* **Julie** *by the elbow inside the house.*

John/Barbara   Wait. I've just one thing to say to you.

David/Julie   What's that?

John/Barbara   Don't get married.

Scene Nine
Lover's leap

*Birdsong, flowing water, sunshine through the leaves. The River
Ythan flows along the front of the stage. The far bank is steep and
rocky, a small cliff; tufts of vegetation grow out of the front of it,
and there is a small ruined building at the top.* **David** *and*
Julie *are near the bottom, climbing slowly upwards. They keep
moving throughout the scene, right out above the audience if
possible.* **Julie** *knows the handholds, leads the way.*

David Are you sure about this?

Julie Trust me. I did it hundreds of times when I was
a kid.

David Aye, but you were young and swack then.
You're an old stiffie these days.

Julie If only I could say the same about you.

David I heard that. What did you say?

Julie I said okay, I'll give up the Grolsch and the Jack
Daniels and the Bloody Marys and the Buds and the
wine and the peach schnapps, I'll go back to ginger beer
and milk with a drop of tea the morn. If you do too.

David It's funny, I suddenly can't hear you any more.

Julie Your lugs are good for that, eh?

David As I was saying, I suddenly can't hear you any
more.

Julie (*pause*) You used to hear everything I said. You
used to come closer if you couldn't hear me right.

David (*indicating that they're on different bits of the
cliff*) Well I can't come closer to you now, can I.

Julie You never can, these days.

David Well, I don't need to any more, cause I ken
what you're going to say, don't I. It was different when

we first went out, we didn't ken each other: everything you said was new and out of the blue. But now I've heard it all afore, I know what you're going to say afore *you* do even. I don't need to listen to you any more.

Julie   That's terrible.

David   I kent you were going to say that.

Julie   No, but seriously. You have to keep listening, otherwise, otherwise ... Christ, we might as well all be talking to ourselves.

David   Look at my mum and dad. They haven't really listened to each other for twenty-five year, and they still get on fine. It's not a problem.

Julie   Well I think it is, if ...

David   Which is more than I can say for this fucking cliff. I'm stuck!

Julie   (*looking over at his pitch*)   You just have to get over to the left a bit, use your knees to kind of grip onto the rock and then just stretch.

David   (*he does what she said*)   And me with all my new Benetton gear on, fuck! What is it we're supposed to be looking at anyroad?

Julie   This is Lovers' Leap. It's out of an old story. There's a ruin on top, you'll see it when we get there. Me and Drew used to call it The Castle when we were wee, but it's not really that.

David   What is it, a pigsty or something?

Julie   No, it was some kind of watchtower but ... (*They should be getting near the top by this time.*) The story is, there was this lassie, right, the laird's daughter, and she was really in love with this young guy. The miller. But her old man wouldn't let them see each other, cause he was just a peasant, and she would inherit all the land for miles around. Well one day the lassie goes to her father and says, Cut me out of your will, father, for I want to get married and live with the man I love. Fine, says the father, for the Laird of Fetterlear's coming over to see's the morn, and I've promised he can have you for a wife. Never, says the daughter, he's an old scrunty man, and anyway, it's the miller I love: I'm eloping! But afore she can run, her father grabs her and drags her away and shuts her up in the tower at the top of this cliff. And there you'll stay till the morn's morn, he laughs, when you'll marry the Laird of Fetterlear! And now I'm away to run that miller off my land once and for all. The lassie looks out of her window, down at the rocks and the river way below. What am I going to do? she cries . . .

Drew (*appearing through the trees at the bottom of the cliff*) Jump!

David Jesus Christ man, you just about had me off there!

Julie What do you want, you big galoot?

Drew Hope you've a head for heights, Davy.

David Ach, this is nothing. Offshore there's a hundred things worse than this.

Drew Aye, like all that five-star grub you have to eat: must be terrible for you.

David No, like hanging upside down from a girder in a force ten gale. I've done that. When it's your job you have to. (*He tries to do a bit of climbing, but then gets nervous and stops.*)

Julie What are you needing anyway, you gype?

Drew Ach, it doesn't matter.

David No, what?

Drew Mind that old cottar house up by the forestry plantation?

Julie   Where dad let old Wattie bide?

Drew   Aye, I've been meaning to demolish it for ages, just to get that corner of the park clear. I was needing you to come and give's a hand to take the windows and the rickle of furniture out first.

Julie   We could help you later on.

Drew   Nah, it's okay, David told me about how you had to get back to town early and that.

Julie   Eh?

David   That's right. Maybe some other time.

Drew   Och aye, there's no hurry. Next time you're out maybe. (*He leaves.*) If you're not back by four I'll send for the mountain rescue.

Julie   What's going on? We were meant to bide till the morn's morn, try and get on better terms with my brother.

David   Ach, what's the point?

Julie   What?

David   He's like you: makes up his mind like that (*Snaps fingers.*) then he's stubborn as a pig stuck in a pipe.

Julie   So?

David   It was just making you miserable being here, I could tell, so I thought it'd be better if we headed back to town.

Julie   For God's sake! Thanks for deciding for me!

David   We're getting married, you'd better get used to it.

Julie   I'll make up my own mind when I leave here, I don't need you telling me! I like Ythanbanks, it still feels like home, though everybody says it's not. I don't need you dragging me away after five minutes.

David What's the point of staying? You just play the same old games with Drew, you don't really talk.

Julie (*sarcastically*) Not like *we* talk, eh?

David Aye, exactly.

Julie Well I don't ken if we do any more.

David I booked a table at that Chinese Olympic place for thenight. We can talk there.

Julie Typical! You're always deciding things for the both of us, and not even asking me about them!

David I could cancel it.

Julie That's not the point!

David Christ woman, you're never happy! You're pissed off cause I don't talk to you, and then the one time I specially arrange it so we *can* have a good long talk – you're pissed off at me for doing that too! I can't win!

They start climbing the cliff again here, but there's no pleasure in it any more, they just have to do it.

Julie This isn't about winners and losers.

David That's funny, you were keen enough to win that argument about who was going to stay offshore.

Julie That's cause it wasn't a proper argument, it was just ridiculous. Of course it has to be me stays offshore: I've got the training, the prospects, the big wages.

David The ovaries.

Julie *What?*

David But I'm just a roustabout, eh? Just a North Sea scaffie?

Julie Look, you ken only one of us can work on the rig after this so-called marriage . . .

David   Okay, but only one of us can have babies.

Julie (*pause*)   What's that supposed to mean?

David   Well, you say *now* that you like your work offshore . . .

Julie   I do. (*She scrambles up onto the top of the cliff.*)

David   You say it makes sense for me to give up the one stab at a decent paying job I have, it makes sense for me to be back on the sites at a hundred quid a week or something . . .

Julie   You could get something better than that!

David   You say these things now, but what's going to happen when you fall pregnant? Will you still want to go back offshore after that? The ROV joystick in one hand and jiggling the pram in the other?

Julie   I don't believe you're saying this.

David   Ken what I think? Drew chucked you off the farm, and now you're getting your revenge on him by chucking me off the rigs!

Julie   You self-centred two-faced macho shithead!

David   It's like my dad says: you can't win with a woman, cause once they're beaten they just start calling you names. And after that . . . it's bursting out greeting. Give me a hand up will you.

She does, he reaches the top, looks around.

Julie   I've never heard you speak such rubbish.

David   Well you should've listened better.

Julie   Aye, I think I should.

David   So this is it, is it? The famous Lovers' Leap. We climbed all that way just to see this pile of shit.

Julie   Aye this is it, this is where we've got to. And the lassie in the old story threw herself off here, plunged to her death on the rocks below, rather than marry someone she didn't love.

David But this is 1993, things don't happen like that any more.

Julie No; now we're the lovers, and *this* is the leap. (*She goes to the edge of the cliff and climbs all the way down with amazing skill in about five seconds flat.*)

David Julie, come back, come back when I tell you! How do I get fucking down from here? Come back!

But she is already walking away along the bank of the river.

Scene Ten
Danger

Back offshore. **Grant** *is sitting in the smoko shack, looking at a newspaper.* **Julie** *is just along from him, having a cup of tea; she looks preoccupied, morose almost, but it's impossible to ignore someone for ever in such a small space.*

Julie I heard some guy got killed yesterday over at Delta.

Grant Aye, I heard that too.

Julie A big swell caught the supply ship and he was crushed atween two containers.

Grant (*shrugs*) Ah well, life goes on.

Julie His doesn't.

Grant (*shrugs again*) His doesn't. But mine does.

From out of nowhere (the top of the cliff from the last scene, actually), **David** *swings in on a winch, high up. As the rope stops swinging, he climbs up a few metres, takes out a hammer from his belt, and starts battering at a rusty bit of panel there.* **Grant** *looks up from where he is sitting, and shouts out an order* *above the rising sea and wind noise.*

Grant   Not there Mitchell! Higher up!

Julie   Did you say something there?

Grant   When you come down to it, the North Sea's not really that dangerous a place to work.

Julie   Really?

Grant   I mean you're more at risk on a building site, or on a farm! How many teuchters get drowned in slurry tanks or crushed under tipping tractors every year?

Julie   Well, too many. Any's too many.

Grant   And how about the stress? Farmers've got the highest suicide rate for any job there is! That's a fact! Out in the so-called peaceful countryside. But listen to this: Aberdeen has the lowest suicide rate for any city in the whole of Britain. Why? Cause so many Aberdonians have good well-paid jobs in the oil industry. Don't talk to them about danger and death: this is the life!

Wind and sea noises fill the theatre. **David** *has got a grinder and is working on the corroded metal with it. Sparks go flying all around.*

Grant   (*leaping to his feet*)   I hope you've got a hot-work permit for that, Mitchell.

David   What?

Grant   Have you got a permit?

David   For the grinder? Aye. Have you got a permit for sending me up here in this wind?

Grant   (*quietly*)   I don't need one.

David   What?

Grant   No slacking now. I'm needing that sealed and painted before the shift ends.

David *shouts something, but the wind drowns him out.* **Grant** *returns to his newspaper.* **Julie** *leans over and taps the page he's reading.*

Julie   So was there anything in there about the death at Delta?

Grant   You're joking!

Julie   The usual whitewash.

Grant   Rubbish! It's just, well, what's the point in getting folk back on the beach all worried? One death in the paper and they get the idea it's Russian roulette out here. You see, it doesn't make the papers when there's *no* incidents for weeks on end.

Julie   Aye Mr Grant, you're a good company man.

Grant   I'm just an ops controller, I'm no company man.

Julie   Yet!

Grant   Keep going Julie, flattery'll get you everywhere.

Julie (*pauses for a second to show she's ignoring his innuendo*) You have to admit, you're a man that usually takes the company line.

Grant   I make up my own mind, based on the things I see – and how much I'm getting paid when I see them.

Back to **David** *on the rope. He is swaying about now in the increasingly strong wind, but still trying to paint the bit of metal he's working on.*

Grant   Hoi, you missed a bit!

David   What?

Grant   Be more careful, you missed a bit!

David   I can't hear you.

Grant   What?

David   I'm chucking this in. The wind's too strong. The paint's getting blown all over the shop.

Grant   I told you Mitchell, that has to be finished this shift. Stay where you are till I tell you.

David   Permission to plunge to my death, sir?

But **Grant** *is back in the smoko again.*

Julie   So offshore isn't a dangerous place to work then?

Grant   There's only about twenty folk a year get killed offshore. On average. I mean some years the figure is higher . . .

Julie   Like 1988.

Grant   Eh, aye.

Julie   It was twenty a minute for a while there.

Pause. **Finn** *walks in.*

Finn   I've just been watching a stoater of a film. You should've seen it Julie.

Grant   Nah, Julie's been too busy organising a new sit-in.

Finn   What?

Grant   Sit on my face, I said, Fine! But don't get fucking political with me.

Julie   He's talking shite.

Grant   Nah, she just about had me signing up for the OILC!

Julie   It's lies Finn: I was thinking aloud, that's all. You ken me, I just like to get on with my work – though half the time some bastard's trying to stop you. Hih, I mind this science teacher I had at the school. I'd been choosing my highers, see, and he calls me in: 'Miss

Allardyce, I see you've opted for higher physics and chemistry.' 'Aye. Are my marks not good enough?' 'Oh there's no problem there, it's just ... would you not be better off studying biology? I always think it's a much more *feminine* science.'

Finn   What's that got to do with safety stuff?

Julie   Everything.

Grant   Nothing.

Finn   Here's what I think: I think there's a lot of bullshitters on the beach that don't give a toss about us working out here. They drive about in their cars, they switch on their central heating, they fry up their bacon and beans – and the thought of folks in the middle of the North Sea drilling up the oil and gas they're using, it never enters their head. And then one day a chopper ditches, or there's a gas leak, or a platform comes adrift in a gale, and, oh dear me, suddenly they're up in fucking arms, getting themselves in a fuck of a state, shooting their mouths off! And why? Cause they feel fucking guilty! Cause ninety-nine per cent of the time they don't even think of us. Cause a hundred per cent of the time they're gobbling up the stuff we produce – they're keeping us out here! Fuck them!

Julie   Aye, serve them right if we all die! Three cheers for chocolate fireguards!

Grant   Keep things in perspective, I say. Okay, a couple dozen folk offshore get killed, but how many people are killed in road accidents in the same time? Thousands!

Julie   So what are you saying, we should all give up our cars?

Grant   No, just folk on the beach: before they start

lecturing us about oil-deaths, *they* should give up *their* cars.

Julie   That'll never happen.

Finn   Aye, and just as well, or we'd be out of a job.

Grant   And talking of jobs, I'm away for a crap.

Finn   You should check out the video. *Driller Thriller*, it's called. I thought it was about a toolpusher that goes psycho and batters everybody to death with a pipe joint. But nah, it was a dentist who put all these women patients under the gas, then laid the reclining chair out and put fillings in all kinds of strange places!

Grant *has left by this time, and* **Julie** *isn't listening, so* **Finn** *shuts up.*

Julie *(she should start saying this before* **Finn** *finishes his last speech)*   The problem is, you can't measure grief; you can't pour it out like a gallon of petrol, or a barrel of crude. It's infinite. One mother whose bairn dies suffers all the grief there is. No less grief if it's a one off and not one in twenty, or one in a thousand. Any amount of death means the same thing: absolute grief. All the grief there is. Too much.

Finn   For fuck's sake Julie, cheer up, give us a smile. The women in the film all had great smiles – course, it was about a dentist.

Julie   Finn, I don't like that crap, it's not realistic.

Finn   Aye, exactly, that's what's so good about it! Come on: you're not bad looking when you smile, you know.

Julie   What?

Finn   Tell you what, come back to my bunk and I'll act out the plot of the film for you.

Julie   You act it out? What did you say it was, *The*

Muppet Movie?

Finn No, it was one of those Dutch imports, know what I mean?

Julie One of those! *The Incredible Shrinking Man*, then?

Finn Christ, have you got a problem Julie Allardyce?

Julie Aye, I'm surrounded by arseholes and pricks.

Finn So was the girl in the film.

Julie Fuck off.

Finn Christ, you have to watch yourself in this place: you're in danger of getting your head bitten off at any fucking moment.

Julie gets up to leave, but just then **David** *staggers in, soaking wet, windswept, covered in flakes of rusty metal and paint splashes. He slumps into a seat.*

Julie Jesus, they didn't have you out in this shit did they?

David Half-way out the flare boom.

Julie (*putting her hand on his shoulder*) You're having a hard time of it these days, eh? Stuck up crumbling cliffs, or dangling off the platform in a raging gale!

David (*putting his hand on top of hers*) I didn't ken you cared.

Julie Despite everything, I do.

She looks him in the eye, but then breaks away and leaves the room. **Finn** *stares after her in amazement.*

Finn Fuck's sake! One minute she's ripping my throat out, next she's treating you like her bosom buddy. What's your fucking secret?

David My secret? Oh! Eh . . . I'll tell you when you're a bittie older Finn.

Scene Eleven
Away and play with your joystick, Grant

We are in the darkened ROV control module. **Julie** *is looking at the videos, etc.* **Grant** *sidles up behind her. (Again the screen is represented by a portable light. During the course of the scene,* **Julie** *shines it on herself, or in* **Grant***'s face or groin at appropriate moments.)*

Grant Wedlock is a padlock, Julie.

Julie What?

Grant Wedlock is a padlock. It's a song.

Julie I never heard it.

Grant That would explain it then.

Julie *(facing him)* Explain what?

Grant Why you're being stupid enough to get married to that no-hoper Mitchell.

Julie *(hiding her anger by turning away)* I don't ken what you're talking about.

Grant You must think I'm thick as shit.

Julie I wouldn't say you were as thick as it . . .

Grant *(he seizes the light, and shines it in her face)* I've got eyes, you know. I can see what's going on. You're lucky I haven't reported the pair of youse yet. (**Julie** *ignores him, so he continues, moving the beam of light up and down her body.*) I thought we could maybe come to some kind of an arrangement. I'll keep quiet about you and Mitchell, if you . . . well . . . we could sort out the details later on.

Julie *(taking the light back)* I could report you for that. Sexual harrassment.

Grant And if you did, I'd have to explain to the company why we were on that subject in the first place.

It'd be a shame, cause you're good at your job, eh?

Julie Aye.

Grant You like it, eh?

Julie Aye.

Grant More than you like Mitchell, or about the same?

Julie (*looking him in the eye*) Me and David Mitchell are friends, nothing more. And me and you have to work together, and there's never going to be more to it than that. Okay?

Grant (*starting to leave*) Wedlock is a padlock, Julie ... but if you ever want it opened, remember me: I'm the man with the key to fit your lock.

Julie (*under her breath, but viciously*) Away and play with your joystick.

Grant (*coming back in, angry*) What was that Allardyce?

Julie I was just thinking it's funny how some ROV operators call their machines 'she'. 'I'm just going to put her into the moonpool,' they say. 'She's a bad tempered bitch theday.' I never understood it.

Grant So what do you call yours then, 'big boy'?

Julie No, I don't call it he or she or anything. It's just a lump of metal, a lump of metal with a lot of clever stuff inside it, but nothing more. It's not a person I'm steering around down there, it's just a lump of machinery. But that's it, you see! Most of the other ROV pilots I've met, they wish it was a person they were controlling. They're out here a fortnight at a time, and meanwhile, what's their wife or their girlfriend getting up to onshore? The old North Sea widow syndrome! You ken what I'm talking about Mr Grant! So these guys get out here and they grab the joystick and they waggle it about like fucking crazy bastards, and all the time they're shouting, 'Come on you bitch, do what you're told!' and 'Christ she's a sluggish hoor this one!' and I just sit here and . . . laugh. It's pathetic, Mr Grant, pathetic.

Grant (*checks watch*)   I don't have the time for this Allardyce.

Julie   Pity.

Grant *leaves, slamming the door.* **Julie** *smiles and turns back to her work.*

Scene Twelve
Navigator

Back onshore. It is the last night of **David** *and* **Julie***'s last onshore fortnight unmarried. In the morning they'll go offshore for a fortnight, and at the end of that they'll be getting married. So both are out with their friends, celebrating. Meanwhile,* **Drew** *is looking after* **Derek***; we don't see him, but from somewhere up in the darkness, his voice emerges, singing a lullaby.*

Drew
There once was a troop of Irish dragoons
Came marching down through Fyvie O
And the captain's fell in love with a very bonnie lass
And her name it was called pretty Peggy O

He hums for a bit, starts making up his own words:

Peggy was bad, she didn't like her dad
And she lived by herself in a castle O
When the soldier came her way, she told him he
    could stay
And his name it was called Captain Andrew O . . .

Lights up on **Julie** *and* **Angela** *marching along Aberdeen beach, singing, and drinking from bottles of beer.*

Julie *and* **Angela**

Now there's many a bonnie lass in the Howe of
    Auchterless
There's many a bonnie lass in the Garioch O
There's many a bonnie Jean in the town of Aberdeen
But the flower of them all is in Fyvie O

Julie It's funny, I hated this when they made us sing
it at the school . . .

Angela I hated everything they made us do at the
school.

Julie . . . but I quite like it now. Or at least I don't
like it, but I understand what it's about.

Angela Except I keep imagining the mannie Urquhart,
his beard sticking out over the top of the piano,
pounding away.

Julie 'Give it some oomph, girls!'

Angela He always liked you, eh, Urquhart?

Julie He always gave me the creeps, the old perv. On
the way out of the class he'd put his arm around my
shoulder and say, 'And here is the bonnie lass herself!'

Angela Jandies!

Julie Some things never change.

Angela But there was a few teachers at the school that
liked you, eh? And you liked them . . .

Julie Well, I went along with them I suppose. But just
to get what I wanted in the end.

Angela It was always me that was the rebel, me that
hated the world, that wanted to smash the place up. I
wanted to throw acid in everybody's face. But you were
all for the world and getting on in it, and all for people
and getting on with them. Me, I painted my bedroom
black and grew my fringe down over my eyes. So I

wouldn't have to look at anybody, and nobody could see me.

Julie   That's the next verse! It's
'Come down the stair pretty Peggy my dear
Come down the stair pretty Peggy O
Come down the stair, comb back your yellow hair
Take a last farewell of your daddy O'

Angela (*while* **Julie** *is singing, so that only the audience hears*)   But here we are a few years later and it's all different, it's the opposite. I've got Derek, and I love him. I worry about the future and what the world's going to be like for him. I want it to be a nice place for when he's growing up. But you, you Julie Allardyce, you're digging tons of black poison out of the seabed, and you don't give a damn: you're painting the *world* black.

Julie   What are you saying Ange?

Angela   Och, I was just thinking about Derek.

Julie   Who's babysitting thenight anyroad?

Angela   It's ... hih. Nobody you'd ken.

Angela *and* **Julie** *wander off. From above them as they go, comes the sound of* **Drew** *softly whistling a verse of the song. Then he's drowned out as* **David** *and* **Finn** *come breenging on, cans in hand.* (*Remember:* **Finn** *doesn't know about the marriage yet, or about* **David** *and* **Julie**'s *relationship at all.*)

Finn   Once I've paid up my fucking house, you'll not catch me offshore. I'll jack that in and never go near the fucking sea.

David   It wouldn't be so bad if you could move around a bit. Follow the sun, ken? It's just being stuck in the one place that's the bastard.

Finn   Ah-ha! (*Starts to change direction, then stops and carries on as before.*) Ach, it's just the seamen's mission. I thought it was a fucking bar.

David   I ken: I'll get myself a boat! A boat with a

bunk bed and a wee cooker and everything. Just the ticket. Then head off into the wild blue yonder: point the nose of the thing for the equator and cheerio!

Finn Where the fuck's that pub from last time? What's it called? The Schooner . . .

David (*pushing open a shopdoor. They are in a ship's chandler's*) Quick, in here . . . (*Pointing at wall behind* **Chandler**.) I want some of those.

Chandler Charts?

David Aye.

Chandler Where of?

David The Sargasso Sea. Zanzibar, North-West Iceland, Honolulu, the Great Barrier Reef, Van Dieman's Land, the Amazon Basin, Timbuctoo, Montego Bay . . .

Chandler We only stock British coastal charts.

David You're joking?

Chandler Sorry.

Finn Call yourself a fucking . . . a fucking . . .

Chandler Ship's chandler.

Finn Aye, well . . .

David Never mind Finn, forget it. (*To* **Chandler**.) Here, do a bit of navigating for us pal: how do we get to the Schooner Bar?

Back with **Julie** *and* **Angela**.

Julie But 'A soldier's wife I never shall be
A soldier shall never enjoy me O
For I never do intend to go to a foreign land
So I never shall marry a soldier O'

Angela Oh 'A soldier's wife you never shall be

For you'll be the captain's lady O
And the regiments shall stand with their hats into
   their hands
And they'll bow in the presence of my Peggy O'

Julie   Bollocks!

Angela   What?

Julie   All this shite about bowing regiments! I don't
believe a word of it! Typical men's lies trying to get into
your pants!

Angela   Do you think it?

Julie   Christ aye: especially coming from a squaddy for
God's sake!

Angela   But does he not die of a broken heart in the
end, the soldier?

Julie   Ach, that's just another lie made up by the
mannie writing the song to get into the pants of
whoever he was singing it till!

Angela   You're just bitter and twisted Julie Allardyce.

Julie   No, I'm just being realistic. You've been away
from men over long Angie, you're forgetting what
they're like.

Angela   Who says I've been away from men?

Julie   Well you never said anything to me about any
man!

Angela   I have my reasons.

Julie   Secrets, eh? It's David: you've been having a
mad affair with him behind my back!

Angela   No!

Julie   That's a shame.

Angela   Eh? What way is that to talk when you're a

fortnight off getting married to him? I thought it was meant to be the happiest day of your life!

Julie Och, I don't know. I suppose every couple has their arguments, eh? I mean it's a stressful time! But still . . .

Angela What's the problem, not enough sex?

Julie (*changing the subject*) The colonel he cries, 'Now mount boys mount . . .'

Angela It is not enough sex!

Julie No, it's not that, it's . . . hey, don't change the subject. If you haven't been seeing David, who is it that's such a big secret?

Angela Och . . . You don't ken him.

Drew *sings from the darkness again, quietly, tenderly.*

Drew
Now there's many a bonnie lass in the Howe of Auchterless
There's many a bonnie lass in the Garioch O
There's many a bonnie Jean in the town of Aberdeen
But the flower of them all is in Seaton O

Back with the lads. **Finn** *standing still,* **David** *walking slowly in circles around him, drinking.*

Finn Tell you what, David. If you're wanting a life on the ocean wave, you could get a job on one of the standby boats.

David Oh Jesus.

Finn They'd let you into that no bother: half of their crews make roustabouts seem like brain surgeons!

David Wise the head.

Finn What?

David That has to be the worst fucking job in oil.

You're on for a month at a time, spewing your ring with seasickness the whole time!

Finn You were the one who wanted onto a fucking boat.

David Aye, but going somewhere, that's the whole fucking point, not just bumping round and round a fucking platform for a month at a time! I was needing to be moving somewhere, not just sticking in one place. (*Drinks.*) Anyway, I've changed my mind. I'll stay working where I am but, but, go on more fucking holidays! (*Drinks again.*) Christ, on the standbys you're not even *in* one place, you're just going round and round a place, bobbing up and down. It's like driving round and round the Mounthoolie roundabout for a month – throwing up in a galeforce wind!

Finn The only boat I'm interested in is steamboats. Come on give me the fucking bottle.

David (*passes the whisky over*) You'll fucking damage yourself pal.

Finn Aye, but in approximately (*Checks watch.*) ten hours' time we'll be starting another shift of enforced fucking sobriety, so within a fortnight I'll be totally healthy again.

David Just in time to come back onshore and get wrecked again.

Finn Exactly. Now pass me the fucking whisky.

David I already did.

Finn Oh aye!

Both laugh.

Back with the women, drunker than ever now.

Angela

But the colonel he cries 'Now mount boys mount'

Julie

And the captain replies 'Oh tarry O
Oh gang nae awa for another day or twa
Till we see if this bonnie lass will marry O'

Angela *and* **Julie**

It was early next morning that we rode away
And oh but our captain was sorry O
The drums they did beat over the bonnie braes of
   Gight
And the band played 'The Lowlands of Fyvie O'

Long ere we won into Old Meldrum town
It's we had our captain to carry O
And long ere we came into bonnie Aberdeen
It's we had our captain to bury O

*Both burst into mostly fake tears and sobs of sorrow, which
quickly change to mostly real laughter. They drink some more beer
and calm down.*

Angela Do you think that really happened?

Julie It's just a song. Do you think 'Bohemian
Rhapsody' really happened?

Both of them think for a while, mouth the words to themselves.

Angela Suppose not, eh?

Julie Nah.

Angela But do you think anybody could ever love
somebody else that much?

Julie Nah.

Angela (*presses quiz-show buzzer*) Wehhhh! That was the
wrong answer Miss Allardyce. The right answer was,
'Yes Magnus, if my David left me, of a broken heart I
would surely die.'

Julie (*thinks*) I would be sad for a while.

Angela Sad?

Julie I mean I've got used to having him around: you have your job, and your car, and your place to bide – and you have your man to take back to the place you bide. Aye, I'd miss him.

Angela There must be more to it than that though! (**Julie** *shrugs*.) Like, a minute after leaving him, you're already thinking about the next time you'll meet? Like, when you're with him, you seem to be seeing funny things going on all around – walking down Union Street and the faces of the folk passing by just constantly make the pair of you burst out laughing? Or suddenly you start noticing what a fine-looking place Aberdeen is – wow, you say, look at the sun on the side of that flats, it's like they're made of solid gold!

Julie I don't know about that.

Angela Like you have twice as many baths as usual! You wash the dishes after your tea in case he comes round. Your bed, that always seemed just the right size for you to stretch out in, well, now it feels like it's way too big and empty . . . when he's not in it with you . . .

Julie Angela, who is this guy you're seeing?

Angela It's your brother, Drew.

Faint light up on **Drew**, *sitting up high, looking happy.*

Drew And her name it was called pretty Angie O.

In a bar.

David To be honest Finn . . . well.

Finn What?

David There's something I have to tell you.

Finn You can't be pregnant, we were always so careful!

David Fuck off.

Finn What then?

David Well . . . it's my round I think.

Finn I know whose round it is: it's mine. Sit down!

David Oh fuck, maybe I shouldn't, I mean . . . it's kind of secret.

Finn You can trust me with a secret! Come on, tell! You can trust me. Anyway, if you don't tell me I'll break your arm.

David Okay, okay. But I'm only telling you cause . . .

Finn . . . cause we're mates. I know, you don't have to . . .

David . . . cause I'm blootered.

Finn You cunt!

David But I will tell you. It's this. I'm not going to be sailing away anywhere.

Finn How?

David I'm well and truly stuck in the one place. Settled down in one place, you might say.

Finn Eh?

David I'm getting married.

Finn What!

David Aye!

Finn You fucking dirty dog!

David Aye well. That's me.

Finn You kept that quiet you dog, you fucking dark

horse! Christ, you never even mentioned you were shagging anybody! Any time the subject came up you always kept your gob shut – I was beginning to think you were the North Sea's first queer roustabout. And now this!

David Hih, aye.

Finn So who is the poor unfortunate then? When am I going to meet her?

David You ken her.

Finn Eh?

David It's Julie.

Finn Julie?

David Julie Allardyce. That you work with.

Finn (*after a pause*) Fuck's sake. Julie Allardyce. Does that mean I can't think about her when I have a wank any more?

David Ahhh, you fucking foul bastard . . .

Finn Here, I knew her before you did, in fact it was me that fucking introduced her to you, so don't get fucking possessive about her all of a sudden.

David Just fuck off and buy me a drink will you? It's my fucking stag night after all.

Finn Christ, so it is, fucking magic! Oblivion here we come!

David I'll drink to that.

Back with the women.

Julie Drew?

Angela Aye.

Julie You are joking Angela?

Angela No.

Julie Jesus Christ. (*Realisation.*) And it's him that's babysitting for you now, eh?

Angela Aye.

Julie *strides off across the stage, her face set in fury; she is rushing back to* **Angela***'s flat.* **Angela** *runs along, trying to keep up with her, trying to calm her down.*

Angela I mean I ken it's a big surprise for you – God, *I* was surprised!

Julie Surprised? Is that what you call it?

Angela What would you call it?

Julie How about insane? No? Off your fucking head? Or was it just drunk and desperate?

Angela Julie! Don't be like that! He's great: a good laugh, gets on with Derek really well . . .

Julie You need your head looked at, quine. (*Shakes her head.*) Are you sure it is Drew? I mean – handy with the bairn, good to get on with? – it doesn't sound like my brother to me.

Angela I was saying to Andrew just the other day, me and him always hated each other when we were bairns. I'd come round to visit you, and he'd always be hanging around, ken. A real dangleberry! We used to think he was a wee shite.

Julie But he's changed: he's a big shite now.

Angela Nah, but once you get talking to him Julie, he's a really nice guy: you've no idea. He listens to what I'm saying, ken, and he thinks about it, I can see him thinking about it. He doesn't just come out with what he believes and that's the end of it: he listens, and he thinks it over.

Julie   I don't believe this.

Angela   It's true. It was years since I'd seen him, then I bumped into him one day up town. He gave me a lift home, and then we got talking and . . .

Julie   Spare me the details Ange!

Angela   I think he's maybe lonely out at Ythanbanks all by himself.

Julie   Don't make me greet!

Angela   He told me you'd been having rows.

Julie   Did he? I suppose he says I started them all.

Angela   No. He says the two of you are alike. You have these really definite ideas about what you want, what you're doing with your life, and you want the whole world to fit in with your plans. And that's okay till you meet somebody else who's got different ideas, different plans – like when you get talking to Drew – cause then BANG! Big collisions!

Julie (*sarcastically*)   You're fairly getting to be an expert on the Allardyce psychology, Angela. I'm impressed.

They have arrived outside **Angela**'s *block of flats.* **Julie** *stops, looks at* **Angela** *for a second, throws back her head and shouts up at the sky.*

Julie   Andrew Allardyce, show your face!

Angela   He'll never hear you.

Julie   Come down you traitorous bastard!

Angela   Julie, I have to live here.

Julie   You can't hide for ever, Allardyce.

Drew *steps out onto the balcony high above, and peers down at them.*

Drew   Wheesht quine, you'll wake the bairn.

Julie I won't be quiet, I'm having this out with you: come down here!

Drew I can't just leave Derek.

Julie Right, that's it. (*She pushes open the door to the flats and runs in.*)

Angela The lift's out of order, you'll have to . . .

But **Julie** *is gone.*

Angela (*shouts up to* **Drew**, *then rushes after* **Julie**) I don't want a punch-up in my flat Drew, come down and meet her half-way.

Drew I'm always trying to do that, but . . . God's sake.

Angela *has disappeared.* **Drew** *goes inside, and soon all three of them are sprinting back and forth up and down the stairs. The sound of their feet thumping on the concrete of the stairwell echoes thunderously.* **Julie** *suddenly stops, and whips round to face* **Angela**, *who is right behind her.*

Julie You'll be moving out to Ythanbanks to bide next.

Angela We have been talking about that actually.

Julie (*clutching her head in her hand*) Aaaaaaaarrrrrrrrgggggggghhhhhhh!!!!!!!!

Drew (*arriving from above*) What the fuck's going on?

Julie I'll tell you: I've been stabbed in the back by my brother and my best friend of twenty year!

Drew What are you talking about quine?

Julie What a way to spend my hen night!

Angela I thought you'd be happy for us, Julie.

Julie Happy? How can I be happy when I'm burning

up inside? I'm burning, roasting, there's a flare in my
chest. I'm burning with anger or hatred or jealousy or
SOMETHING! I can't stand it, cool me down!

Angela *holds out a bottle of beer and she grabs it, takes a long
drink, then flings the bottle away.*

Julie   What am I drinking – petrol?

Drew (*putting a hand on her shoulder*)   What's got into you
Julie?

Julie   Fuel's got into me, fuel for burning! All my life
I've been filling up, more and more stuff piling up inside
me – my dad and the farm and the work and the shite
from the bears and David, *David* – it all piles up, and
the pressure builds up, and the temperature too till the
stuff you started with's gone, and what you have left is
fuel! Crude! Oil's building up, till you're ready to burst,
building and filling till ... one day ... something gets
you, something drills down into your heart and
BLOWOUT! BLOWOUT! The fuel's jetting out, it's
blowing like a gusher, and it's burning, burning, full of
fuel – and I'm burning!

The scene ends with this shout that is almost a scream.

**Scene Thirteen
Burnt out**

*On the balcony of **Angela**'s flat, shortly after the big row on the
staircase. **Drew** stares out over the sea; **Angela** comes out from
the living-room, shutting the door quietly behind her.*

Angela   She's asleep.

Drew   How about Derek?

Angela   You ken what he's like: if the flats tumbled
down into the sea he'd just yawn and roll over.

Drew   Hih. (*Pause.*) Was she drunk?

Angela   Can you not tell the difference atween somebody blazing with jealousy and somebody bleezing drunk?

Drew   I've never seen her like that afore.

Angela (*embraces him*)   She's never seen you like *this* afore, that's the problem.

Drew   Do you think it?

Angela   It must've been a shock to her.

Drew   I thought she'd like it, ken, her brother and her best friend getting involved; it's kind of like a jigsaw, all the pieces fitting thegether.

Angela   Aye, but she feels like she's the piece left over, the bit that doesn't fit in anywhere . . .

Drew   Her and David, surely they fit thegether . . .

A noise comes up to them from the street below. It is **Finn** *and* **David** *singing drunkenly as they stagger along the road.*

Finn *and* **David**
   There once was a troop of Texas tycoons
   Came driving down through Fyvie O
   And they used their expertise to explore the cold
      North Sea
   And the whole of the countryside went crazy O

   Oh who can resist the feel of siller in his fist
   Who doesn't want work and wages O
   Let the others go to hell, I'm doing fine myself
   And the oil's going to keep us rich for ages O

They wander off down the road. Back to the balcony.

Angela   I'm not sure. Some of the things Julie was saying, I reckon there's trouble brewing there.

Drew   Trouble's never far away from Julie.

Angela You're joking! Julie's the least troublesome person I ever kent! I was the one who was always in the shit at school. I was the one that 'got into truble' with a psycho from Mintlaw. Julie was no trouble at all: always in the top class, straight into that training scheme, passed all the exams, two years offshore being great at her job, and to cap it all she's engaged to this nice-seeming guy who's also earning stacks of cash, who's also got his foot in the door of the whole oil thing.

Drew So what's her problem then? What was all the bawling about?

Angela Her problem is, me and you, we don't have any of that things, but we're still really happy; but Julie, she's got it all, and . . .

Drew . . . she doesn't like it.

Angela Is it not obvious?

Drew To you maybe: you're getting awfully good at working out the thoughts of the Allardyce clan!

Angela (*remembering* **Julie** *said just this earlier on*) You're quite like her really, you know. Exactly like her, except you're the exact opposite. Ken?

Drew You're like her too: speak a terrible hease of shite sometimes.

Angela And you say the nicest things . . . (*They kiss.*) Better go and wake her up, I suppose; she'll want to get her stuff thegether for going offshore the morn. (*She opens the door to the lounge.*)

Drew You do it, you're better at that kind of thing.

Angela God aye, I'm the Red Adair of emotional blowouts. You ken who Red Adair is, eh?

Drew Michty aye. (*Pause.*) Used to dance with Ginger Rogers.

Scene Fourteen
Survival suits

Early morning. In a departure lounge at Dyce heliport. **Julie**,
David, **Finn** *and* **Grant** *are struggling into survival suits,
along with various other workers about to fly offshore. They all
look hungover;* **Julie** *is also approaching an emotional all-time
low, and seems distant from the others' wisecracking.*

Julie   One day I'll find a suit that fits me. (*The one she's
putting on is much too big.*)

David   Once they'd fished you out of the sea they'd
need another half hour to winch you out of the survival
suit.

Finn   'Survival' suits! Who are they trying to kid?
You'd be better off wearing a dinner jacket and white
fucking dickie. At least when they hauled you out of the
sea in a block of ice you'd look the part: a fucking
penguin. (*He does a penguin walk, then falls down onto a
chair.*)

Julie   Who gets the dead man's seat theday then? I'd
take it, but I can't, I'm not a man.

Finn   I'll have it, I'll have it. The way my head feels
this morning, violent death would be a fucking blessing.

Grant   I'm sure that could be arranged, Finlay.

Voice over PA   Flight 126, 126. The departure of this
flight will be delayed by four minutes.

David   Oh shit . . .

Voice   Sorry, that reads forty minutes.

Everybody   Oh shit . . .

Voice   This is due to a helicopter crew shortage.
Thankyou.

Finn   No, thank*you*.

Grant (*as everybody sits down, unzips their suits etc.*) So chopper captains get hangovers as well.

David Aye, I saw him last night outside the Schooner, chucking up into his pilot's hat.

Finn No, that was me with your baseball cap.

David Makes a change from all of us chucking up in the back of his chopper . . .

Grant Typical Aberdeen helicopter company, though. Too tight to hire a spare pilot, eh!

Julie Ha ha.

Grant Here, that reminds me. Did you hear about the Aberdonian toolpusher? His wife wanted to see what it was like flying offshore, so he has a word with the pilot. Here man, I'll slip you a ten . . . a five . . . three quid if you'll give the wife a hurl. Ach, she can come for nothing, says the pilot, just as long as you sit in the back there and don't interrupt me. Keep quiet and it's a freebie! Well, an hour and a half later they touched down up at one of the Brents. I'm amazed, says the pilot, you came the whole way and never said a word. Aye, says the Aberdonian, it was right hard to keep quiet, especially when we went through that bittie turbulence and the wife fell out of the machine!

Finn Here's a good one, right. Fred fae Fitty goes and visits Frankie fae Froghall one Saturday morning, and arrives just in time to see him giving each of his five wee kids a fifty pence bit. Pocket-money time, says Frankie. Five times fifty pence every week of the year! says Fred. That's a hell of an amount of siller by Christmas! Extravagance, man! Ah but, says Frankie, I told them the electricity meter's a piggy bank: the bairns keep us in heat and light all year round!

David Here, this is slander, you bastards!

Grant Ah, we've touched a nerve I think!

Julie It's not slander.

Grant Ah-ha lover boy! *She* has spoken!

Julie It's downright racist, that's what it is.

Finn Away and shite!

Grant Right, there was this Aberdonian working in a shipyard down on the Clyde . . .

David Christ, this must be an old story.

Grant And he gets part of his anatomy cut off by a circular saw.

Julie (*sarcastically*) Ha ha ha.

Grant No, it's his hand, his hand gets cut off. Anyway, the man's about to be rushed to hospital, when the ambulance driver says, Quick, get the sawn-off hand, and we'll maybe be able to sew it back on again. So all the guys in the yard, they start searching for the hand, but they can't find it anywhere, it's lost amongst all the scrap and shite on the floor. And the ambulance driver shrugs, and he's just about to piss off, when one of the guy's mates says, Hold on, I've got an idea: once an Aberdonian, always a bloody Aberdonian. And he takes a ten pence piece out of his pocket and drops it on the floor. Tinkle, tinkle, tinkle . . . And out scuttles the hand, snatches up the money, and grips on tight all the way to the hospital.

David That's enough you bastards. I'll show you some *real* Aberdonian culture: the Dance of the Randy Roughneck.

David *starts singing the 'Stripper' tune, with different voices for different instruments etc. He uses this to accompany a comic dance / strip, during which he peels off his survival suit, with teasing looks over his shoulders, pulling up and down of zips etc.* **Finn** *and* **Grant** *join in singing and clapping; they cheer and shout ('Get them off' etc.) at particularly raunchy moments.*

Grant *in particular tries to involve* **Julie**, *by nudging her, tugging at her zips. She gets increasingly pissed off. Just as* **David** *strips the survival suit off completely, there is an announcement:*

Voice over PA   Attention, attention. Flight 126 is now departing. Please board immediately.

Julie   Thank fuck for that!

Finn   Too right: another thirty seconds and he'd've been down to his Ys!

Grant   Christ, you were pretty fucking sexy there Mitchell, I'm telling you. I'd go for him, wouldn't you Julie?

Julie   No, I don't think I would.

**Scene Fifteen
Accident**

A sunny day out on the rig deck. The green light burns steadily. There is the noise of pulleys, motors, wind, generators. **Julie** *and* **Finn** *are hauling the ROV on board after a job, with* **Julie** *watching the videos as before,* **Finn** *handling the cable etc.* **David** *is nearby, working at some tedious task;* **Grant** *is around somewhere too. There is a fairly long period of nothing happening, just to establish the routine everyday nature of the work in progress. After a while, the ROV rises past the edge of the deck, swings a bit, then stops, the cable loose on the deck beneath it.* **Finn** *manipulates the controls for a few seconds, but nothing happens.*

Julie   What's the problem?

Finn   What?

Julie   Why've you stopped?

Finn   It's not me that's fucking stopped.

Julie Is there a jam?

Finn I reckon it's the fucking docking device.

Julie A failure?

Finn I don't fucking know; it just fucking stopped.

Julie Let me have a look.

Grant (*pauses as he passes*) What's up?

Finn Some kind of fucking jam.

Julie (*examining the winch, from a safe position*) Maybe the bullet's at an angle and the dogs . . .

Grant Come on, we can't fuck about, we need to get this bastard out the road afore the supply ship arrives.

Julie You think we like it hanging around? There's a jam in the docking device, we're trying to clear it now!

Grant A jam? You should've said! Roustabout, get over here.

David What's going on?

Grant We need a bit of manpower here, we've got a cable jammed. Get up there and give it a yank will you?

Julie Don't go inside the bight . . .

Grant (**David** *pauses, so he gives him a shove, and spits at* **Julie**) Here, you might tell him what to do in the fucking bedroom, but not on my fucking deck, okay?

David Hey . . .

Grant We have to get this cleared! Do it! Now!

David *shrugs, goes over to the ROV, and gives a big tug on its cable. Obviously this does some good, for the motor starts again; but something fails to grip, and the ROV falls a few feet instead of rising. This makes the slack cable tighten suddenly, trapping* **David***'s hand and yanking him up into the air. It happens in an* *instant.* **David** *screams. All of this very fast and confused and noisy.*

Finn   Fuck! Davy!

He runs towards him, then back to the winch controls. The light starts flashing yellow, indicating an alert.

Grant   What the fuck's going on?

Finn   She's jammed again, the bastard fucking . . .

Grant   Mitchell, you stupid cunt!

Julie   David! Get him down! (*Runs over and lifts his feet in her arms, trying to take some of the weight off his hand.*)

Finn   Grant, get a fucking ladder.

Grant   Allardyce, get a ladder here: we have to get this clear . . .

Julie (*taking no notice*)   Finn, we have to slacken the cable.

Finn   There's only one way to do that: drop her over the side.

Julie   Jesus Christ! (*Thinks for a split second, clenched fists to her forehead, but there's only one possible answer for her.*) Go on, ditch the bastard.

Finn   Eh . . . are you sure?

Grant (*having found it himself*)   Here, stand on this ladder.

Julie   He can't stand anywhere, he's fucking unconscious. Finn, cut the umbilical!

Finn   I can't ditch her, I hardly got the chance to fly her yet!

Julie   Ditch it!

Grant   Stop! We'll take the weight of his hand with the ladder, then figure out some way to . . .

Julie   The cable is cutting his hand off!

Finn   Jesus Christ ... Grant, you're a witness to this, I don't want to do it, but ... (*He goes over towards the nearby workshop container.*)

Grant (*blocking **Finn**'s way*)   That's half a million quids' worth of company property!

Julie   It's that or David's hand.

Grant   Just give me a few minutes to think this over.

Finn   I mean I don't want to lose my contract ...

Grant   Aye: now *you* wise the fucking head Allardyce.

Julie (*she runs over and knocks **Grant** away from the front of the container*)   Right, don't bother yourself Finlay, I'll fucking ditch the bastard.

*She grabs a grinder out of the workshop container and starts to cut through the main umbilical cable with it. A shower of sparks flies everywhere. **Grant** watches, appalled, from the deck. **Finn** goes over and supports **David**.*

Grant   You need a hot work permit for that, for God's sake.

Julie   I don't believe you!

Grant (*getting to his feet, trying to stop her working*)   But this is a serious risk to the whole installation here! Every time a grinder is used you need to obtain a ...

Finn   Enough Grant, shut your face and help me.

Grant (*goes to help **Finn**, but is still snarling at **Julie***) You know you'll never work offshore again?

Julie   Me or David?

*The cable is cut. The ROV falls away. **Finn** lowers **David** to the ground.*

Grant   In fact you'll be run off on the next free seat.

Julie   In that case, Grant ... (*On the way over towards* **David**, *pauses for a second and punches him in the face as hard as she can.*) Finn, get onto the fucking medic, will you, and the radio room for a chopper.

Finn (*runs off, shouting into his radio*)   Medivac! Medivac!

Grant   You're finished out here, Julie Allardyce.

Julie   Thank Christ! I'm finished out here! I'm finished!

Immediately cut into full blast helicopter noise, pitch darkness.

Scene Sixteen
No mercy dash

Darkness. Helicopter noise. Lights up on **David** *lying on a stretcher in the back of the chopper.* **Julie** *is sitting beside him. The sound of drumming starts to emerge from under the engine noise, gradually getting louder. The rest of the cast march onto the stage, beating on oil drums and petrol cans, and walls and objects they pass. Their faces are expressionless, hard hats are pulled down over their eyes but the drumming is savage.* **Julie** *watches them for a while, till* **David** *tugs her sleeve, pulls her down towards him, and speaks.*

David   Thanks for being there for me Julie. What an idiot, eh? If it hadn't been for you, aye, and Finn as well I suppose, where would I be now? Grant would've left me hanging there till the seagulls picked my een out. No: he'd've ditched me over the edge to save the machine! So thanks, Julie. Specially cause ... I ken what the ROV meant to you, but you chose me.

He falls silent for a spell. **Julie** *looks at the drummers again. They are now marching in a line, no longer beating on random objects; now they are drumming on the hard hat of the person walking in front of them. Signs of weariness or pain are starting to show on their faces.*

David   What's going to happen to me now, eh? This

won't do much for my typing speed, will it? Anyway, the hand's still there so who cares. It's good you're here to look after me; as long as you love me I'll be okay.

Julie This is it David . . .

David Aye, this is what's really important.

Julie No, what I mean is, I don't love you.

The drummers, who have taken over from the engine noise completely by this time, fall silent.

David What?

Julie I don't love you David. We better finish. No sense in fooling ourselves. It's over.

David Julie, what do you mean?

Julie Do you think I wouldn't've chose Finn over the ROV? Do you think I wouldn't've chose *Grant*? Fuck's sake! I chose you because you're a human being and the ROV's a lump of metal. That's why I chose you. I didn't choose you cause I love you.

David Julie . . .

Julie Cause I don't love you any more.

The dummers start up again, but this time not with a complex clattering; this time they beat out a slow, steady, simple heartbeat rhythm. **Julie** *talks over the top of them, getting up from her seat and striding about the stage, doubling up or leaping about as the emotions of what she's saying dictate.*

Julie You fall in love, or you dive into love. Either way it's a splash zone. For six months or a year you're battered about, tossed this way and that – you're up on the peaks and down in the troughs – but all the time it's raging, it's whirling, it's a wild wild time. A force ten time! You're carried along, rushed along, so fast you can't breathe, and there's spray on your face and wind at your back and sun in your eyes. Like that time we

went surfing up at the Broch! And it feels so wild, you
want it to last for ever, but it's scary as well cause
you're not in control. 'See that sea down there? It's a
big bad bastard and for now it's tossing us this way and
that and we're surfing along and laughing, but any split-
second the big old bastard sea could change its mood
and break us instead, come crashing down on our heads,
big lumps of water crashing and smashing . . .' But
there's no time to worry about that even, cause for now
you're still being swept along, swept along on top of the
waves! Only you're not.

You look around, and something's changed, a year's
passed and you're not up amongst the surf and the sky
any more, you're cruising along through the depths.
You've started to sink, and you never noticed!
Everything's calm, everything's smooth, everything's clear
– but dark. Down you go, deeper and deeper, still
moving forward, but down. From the clear blue water
just under the splash zone, down and down to the dark
green depths, down and down – and still it's calm and
peaceful, no turbulence reaches you now – down to the
black, down to the black deeps of the sea. Of love.
Deep love. Calm love. Dead love! There's all this weight
above you, and it's crushing down upon you. You can't
see where you're going, for you're too far away from the
outside world – up there, the sun, the waves – you're
floating blind through the dark. And after a while it
doesn't matter you're blind, cause you're not moving
anywhere anyway, you've sunk to a stop, you've rooted
in the mud, the mud of the seabed, the mud of the
sexbed, the habit of the sex. You're stuck, you're fucking
stuck, and by the time you realise, you're almost too
late, there's almost no chance whatsoever of escape.

You start to notice the others, the others that mean
you're not alone, you're not special, you're not unusual
even! Oh no, no: there's others, all around. All around
you, stuck in the mud, you hear their mumbles, their

jokes, their pet names, their petty rows and hypocritical reconciliations – you see their tight lips and their white-lying eyes and their same old hug, same old handhold, same old kiss or same old sitting at opposite ends of the sofa, rolling to the outside edges of the bed, one in the pub, one in the kitchen, one with the kids, one with the mates, one in the strums, one in a rage, one in tears, one in torment, the other in torment, both in torment and boredom and hatred and torment and self-hatred and ... that's ... it ... till ... you ... die.

Unless you break free. Kick your feet free. Get out of that mud. Quick, before it reaches your mouth! Before it reaches your brain ... While there's still a chance, break free! 'Come back, look out,' the others say, 'what you're doing's dangerous! Never hear of the bends? Decompression sickness? If you break free of the mud and shoot away up, your blood'll boil into bubbles, your heart'll burst, you'll be dead by the time you get back to the air – *if* the air still exists up there!'

But I don't care, you tell them. That's what I'm saying now: I don't care! I'm going back up, I'm breaking free, I'm heading back up to the air and the light and wild surf. And I'm leaving you David, I'm leaving you, and it breaks my heart, cause I did love you. I loved you, and that's what got us *into* these depths, and the only way out of the depths is to say it, say it, say it: I don't love you, I'm leaving, it's over.

Scene Seventeen
Drumallochie

Sudden change from the noise of the flight to gentle fiddle music. We're at Dyce heliport. **Julie** *helps* **David** *down from the helicopter, but as soon as his feet touch the ground his mother and father grab him, shoving* **Julie** *aside.* **David** *does nothing to stop this. Then* **Drew** *appears and leads* **Julie** *away. He sings the*

whole of the song that he started in Scene 5, again with suitable
fiddle accompaniment. **Julie** *seems numb at first, then joins in,*
singing verse 3 and verse 5. During the course of the song they
move away from the heliport; by the end they are back at
Ythanbanks.

Drew

'Twas on a chill November's night when fruits and
    flowers were gone
One evening as I wandered forth upon the banks of
    Don
I overheard a fair maid and sweetly thus sang she
'My love he's far from Sinnahard and from
    Drumallochie'

I said 'My pretty fair maid, you're walking here alone
Lamenting for some absent one upon the banks of
    Don
Come tell the reason of your grief, come tell it all to
    me
And why you sigh for Sinnahard and for
    Drumallochie'

Julie

'Oh Peter was my true love's name upon the banks of
    Don
He was as fine a young man as e'er the sun shone on
But the cruel wars of Scotland they have parted him
    from me
And now he's far from Sinnahard and from
    Drumallochie'

Drew

I said 'My pretty fair maid, come give to me your
    hand
For on the bonnie banks of Spey I have both house
    and land
And I will share it all with you if you will be my
    bride

And you'll forsake the bonnie lad that lived upon
    Donside'

Julie

Says she 'Kind sir, your offer's good but I must it deny
And for the sake of my true love alone I'll live and
    die
And for the space of seven years jet black shall cover
    me
For him who lived at Sinnahard near by
    Drumallochie'

Drew

But since my love was weeping I could no longer
    stand
I clasped her in my arm and said 'Oh Betsy know
    your man
Behold your faithful Peter now he's free from every
    care
And on the bonnie banks of Don we've met to part
    no more'

Julie *and* **Drew**

'Aye, on the bonnie banks of Don we've met to part
    no more'

*The fiddle continues for a short time, blending in with birdsong,
the sound of the Ythan, etc.* **Julie** *and* **Drew** *come to a halt.*

Julie I loved it when granny and granda sang that.

Drew They're real places, you ken, Sinnahard and
Drumallochie, up by Kildrummy, that's what's so good
about it.

Julie I don't know what's so good about it, but ...
Drew, ken Wattie's cottar house up in the lee of the
plantation?

Drew Aye.

Julie Did you knock it down yet?

Drew No, I never got round to emptying it even. Do

you want to give's a hand to do that the now?

Julie Not exactly.

The fiddle starts up again, while **Julie** *and* **Drew** *walk on. They enter the old house, shoving the door open, coughing at the dust.*

Drew The power's off at the mains.

Julie Open those shutters, will you?

Drew *opens the shutters, and bright light comes pouring in through the window, leading into the next scene.*

Scene Eighteen
A wedding

The Wedding March blasts out on a grand organ. Arched doors at the back of the stage are flung open, and the music gets even louder as people spill out of the kirk. In the middle of the steer is a bride in a big white dress and a groom in a kilt get-up. The lights behind them are so bright that they are more or less silhouetted, and for a while we can't make out who they are. Folk throw confetti over the happy couple, and flashes go off as photos are taken. Everybody is laughing and cheering and shouting. Now the lights from the kirk dim, and we can see that it is **Drew** *and* **Angela** *that have been getting married. They are surrounded by the whole cast, including* **Julie** *and* **David**.

The rig lights start to come up, and also the lights for the river and trees at Ythanbanks. Gradually the cast splits up into separate groups, with **David** *and* **Finn** *and* **Grant** *back on the rig, going through the docking dogs routine that* **Julie** *and* **Finn** *did early on. Elsewhere there are drummers drumming, somebody climbing the Lover's Leap cliff, somebody else playing 'The Bonnie Lass o'Fyvie' on a fiddle.* **Drew** *and* **Angela** *pass from one group to the next getting congratulations from each one.*

Only **Julie** *is by herself. She also passes from one group of folk to the next, but she doesn't interact with them, just looks at them* *and moves on. When she has visited each group, she comes up to the front of the stage and sings, her voice rising clear above the clashing noises and music behind her.*

Julie

Now there's many a bonnie lass in the Howe of
  Auchterless
There's many a bonnie lass in the Garioch O
There's many a bonnie Jean in the town of Aberdeen
But the flower of them all bides at Fyvie O

Blackout.

One Sure Thing

Characters

Keith, *mid to late twenties*

One Sure Thing was first performed on 5 November 1994 at the Cottier Theatre, Glasgow, by Castlemilk People's Theatre, directed by Steve Crone, with the following cast:

Keith   Stephen McCole

Keith *is lying on the stage in darkness. Music plays: Hank Williams singing 'I'll never get out of this world alive'. After the first three verses and bridge, during the instrumental break, the music fades away till it's barely audible. Simultaneously, lights come up on the actor. He speaks.*

The first thing that comes into my head when I wake is, 'Thank Christ, I'm alive! I could've died in the night but I didn't, I'm alive.' (*He sits up.*) That's when my problems start: that's when I think, 'I didn't die in the night, so it could be any time today, any time now.' (*A pause, as if he's waiting for it to strike him.*) There's no way out. If you're dead you're dead, if you're alive you're going to be dead. If you don't go during the night, you'll go during the day. Some day, any day.

Hank Williams fades up again, for the bridge and verse after the instrumental. He gets up and walks around a bit. Music fades out before the song ends.

One night I was sitting on the settee watching telly, my two wee boys playing with Lego on the carpet behind me. And then this thing happened. I don't ken if you get it, or if it's just me. Do you get it? What happened was, I realised I'd no earthly idea what I'd been watching on the box. Not just for a minute, but for hours, all night. My mind had been somewhere else all the time, I'd been in a complete fucking limbo, staring at the telly. Then what happened was (*He snaps his fingers.*) I kind of came to. I saw where I was sitting, I looked around the room, and . . . I *needed to see the kids*. 'Gordon, Darren, come here!'
'I'm here Daddy.'
'Me too.'
'Aye, but come round here, where I can see you.'
'Och . . .'
'Come here!'
They came round from behind the settee, and stood in front of me. I mind they were in their pyjamas. Ready for . . . (*He jerks his head upwards.*) I took hold of

their hands.

'Are you all right?' I said.

'Aye.'

'Good. Are you sure?'

'We're building a castle.'

'Good, good. But look at me.' They raised their eyes to mine. 'What's the one sure thing?' I said.

They didn't speak. I looked at each of them in turn, trying to get them to understand how important this was. Then I thought, 'Christ, did I say that just then, or did I just think I said it? Have I been in bloody limbo-land again? Is that why they're not replying?' So I gave them a bit of a shoogle each then asked them again: (*Louder.*) 'What's the one sure thing in this life?'

'Going to school,' said Gordon after a second. He's the oldest. P2. 'You have to go to the school,' he says.

I looked at him, I nodded. 'No,' I said. 'You could be sick, or you could be skiving. You're wrong, school isn't sure.' I turned to the younger boy, leant closer to him. I said, 'Darren, how about you? Tell me, wee man, what is the one thing we all know for sure?'

He frowned, then stopped frowning, shrugged his elbows.

'Will I tell you?' I said.

'Aye.'

'The one sure thing is: we're all going to die.'

Darren pulled away, he looked over my shoulder towards the kitchen door. His eyes were beginning to pucker up and fill with tears. 'Mummy!' he says.

'Wheest, wheest!' I go, letting go his hand, and Gordon's too, but the kitchen door's already opening, and Lesley's taking a step in.

'What's up honey?' she says.

'Nothing,' says Gordon. He's older, he's a good boy.

'It's Daddy,' goes Darren, 'he's asking me *questions* . . .'

'Hey, come on son . . .' I stretched out to pat Darren on the head, but he jerked away and ran over behind his mother.

'Keith,' she said, 'what have you been saying to them?'
'Nothing! Nothing at all.' I needed the telly remote
control. I looked around, couldn't see it anywhere.
'Keith, what did you say to upset them?'
'Nothing! Except, well . . .' I looked up, gave her a bit of
a grin. 'Nothing.'
'He said we were going to die,' said Gordon, traitor. 'He
said it was the one true thing.'
'Och, Keith . . .'
'I was just trying to get them thinking, you ken. (*He
laughs, though it seems forced.*) It's good to face up to . . .
things.'
'Not at the age of six and four, though!'
'Well . . . it has to be sooner or later.' *There* was the
remote control on the arm of the settee. It had been in
front of me all the time. I turned up the volume. It was
one of those wildlife programmes. Big animals tearing
little animals to pieces, ken, the usual.
She stared down at me for a few seconds, I could feel
her there, she was staring at me. So I didn't look round.
Then she said, 'Come on boys, time for bed.' For once
they seemed happy to go up.

*Hank Williams sings the first chorus and verse of 'Weary blues
from waitin''.*

It's not that I'm sick. Lesley's not sick. And the boys,
they're bursting with life. But that kind of makes it
worse, ken? Cause it doesn't matter how alive you are
now, that won't help you *then*. (*He walks in a small circle.*)
I'm glad I just stay here all the time. I mean what's the
point of going out and about, running around the town,
trying to kid yourself on it matters? It doesn't matter,
and it doesn't help. Just stay in your house, stay in your
room, stay in your fucking comfy chair. What's the point
of anything else?

*Hank fades in and out for the second chorus and verse of 'Weary
blues'.*

When the kids were settled, Lesley came into the lounge, then went ben the kitchen. She reappeared five minutes later, two cups of coffee and a couple bits of cheese-on-toast on a plate.

'Here you go,' she said.

Me, I was trying to concentrate on the programme.

'Keith.'

'Hmm.'

'I wish you wouldn't speak to the kids like that. Especially just afore they go off to bed. (*Pause.*) Keith, are you listening?'

'What? Aye, aye.'

'Well, I mean to say. You'll be giving them bad dreams.'

I felt a wave of something coming over me: darkness. I turned towards her. 'Bad dreams?' I said. 'I wish it *was* all bloody bad dreams, Lesley!'

She looked at me. 'Have you been worrying about them making a mistake again? You getting buried and then waking up?'

'Christ, not just getting buried, that would be bad enough. But imagine waking up and finding yourself being created. I mean *cremated*: imagine yourself being burned to death! The flames licking up the coffin walls, you banging and shouting as the air gets hotter, but your screams covered up by the roaring of the furnace! Jesus Christ almighty, it makes my blood run cold . . .'

Here's me talking about being cold, but the sweat was fucking lashing off me. I felt like there was a wee crematorium inside me, burning me up from the inside out.

'Keith,' says Lesley, 'you're just not being sensible. I'm sure they do loads of tests and everything. I mean they make sure you really are, you know, *dead*.'

'The autopsy! (*He shouts.*) That's almost worse: lying out there on a cold stone slab, some guy in a white coat slicing you open – slicing you right up the middle! – then cutting out all your innards, your lungs and your heart! (*He mimes all his inner organs being ripped out, with him looking down at the mess, aghast.*) And sometimes they even saw off the top of your head and poke around in your brain! (*He's virtually frothing at the mouth now, he's getting so excited. He wipes his lips with the back of his hand.*) Imagine lying there and feeling all that!'

'You're just being stupid now,' said Lesley, shaking her head. 'You'll be dead: you won't feel a thing.'

'I might.'

'No you won't: that's the whole point of being dead. God Keith, sometimes you're just so . . . Jesus!'

She took a bite out of her cheese-on-toast. When she put it down again, a long string of melted cheddar stretched out between her mouth and the piece. Then it snapped, landed on her chin. Jesus Christ, it made me want to greet.

'I've been thinking about it a lot, and I've got a theory about it: it's just like now, except you're dead. My theory is: (*He slaps himself in the face.*) you feel everything after you die, *everything.*'

I leant over towards her, I was gripping onto the arm of the settee, for fear of falling off and being dragged down and down and down.

'After I die,' I said, (*Slowly.*) 'I'm going to feel every little thing they do to me. That scares me: the fear of dying and being alive. Dying and being alive. (*Not just to her any more, but out front, to everyone:*) Dying. And being alive. Being alive.'

The final chorus of 'Weary blues' fades in. He speaks over the top of the music, repeating the phrase, 'Being alive'. Probably he will say it twelve or thirteen times. The final time he says it should be just as the music ends; the words 'Being alive' are what the audience should be left with.

Rug Comes to Shuv

Rug Comes to Shuv was first performed on 31 May 1996 at the Traverse Theatre, Edinburgh, with the following cast:

Rug	Brian Alexander
Shuv	Kenneth Bryans

Directed by John Tiffany
Lighting by Ben Ormerod

Complete darkness. Thunderously loud music: 'Jailbird' by Primal Scream, from the album Give Out But Don't Give Up. *After the first verse and chorus, fade out the music and fade up lights simultaneously. Over the last ten seconds of music* **Rug** *and* **Shuv** *approach from off, shouting at each other.*

Rug   I am not.

Shuv   You are.

Rug   I am not!

Shuv   You are!

Rug   I AM NOT!

Shuv   YOU ARE!

They walk in, quickly. Both are mid-twenties, both from Edinburgh. What they walk into is **Shuv**'s *bedsit: cramped, filthy, littered with clothes, empty bottles and cans, chip papers and carry-out cartons. It's ten o'clock, Friday night; they're all revved up, talk at a furious pace, with great intensity.*

Rug   I am not fucking your wife.

Shuv (*pause*)   Come on.

Rug   Fuck off.

Shuv   Just once, that'll do.

Rug   Get to fuck you radge, do you think I'm daft? Well I think you're sick.

Shuv   Sick's got fuck all to do with it you stupid cunt. I mean I'm not asking you to fucking *enjoy* it – fuck all chance of that to be honest, that's half the fucking problem – I'm just saying we'll get her bevvied up, *paralytic* right, you stick your cock up her and BINGO I step out with the camera.

Rug   You're a fucking pervert, man.

Shuv (*laughs*)   Well I reckon you must be fucking bent.

Rug Fuck off.

Shuv Here's a chance to get your hole, you cunt, and you're turning it down! I'll tell you, I'll even buy the drink! A bottle of Buckie for her and a few cans for us – not too much, cause we want a fine big stiffie in the pictures.

Rug You're fucking . . . out of the park, man.

Shuv Am I fuck.

Rug Aye, cause I tellt you: you don't have to go through this rigmafuckingrole these days. No one's fucking caring if you want divorced. You just get a lawyer onto it, blah blah blah, three weeks later there you go, mutual fucking consent.

Shuv Ah but, who would get the kid?

Rug Eh?

Shuv This is it, you see. I'm not needing Simone away with her – she's an old fucking alkie! What kind of mother's that for my daughter?

Rug What Shuv, you're a better mother?

Shuv Aye! So I've got to prove she's fucking unfit, right, bad morals and that. Step one, photos prove she's a slag, shags anycunt. Her defence, 'He led me on, your honour, I was drunk.' We jump in, 'She's *aye* fucking drunk, she's a fucking alkie, your honour!' Case closed!

Rug No way.

Shuv Come on.

Rug Nuh.

Shuv I'll pay you. A tenner. (**Rug** *looks away*.) Twenty!

Rug Forget it.

Shuv You are a poof.

Rug I'm not going to do it.

Shuv When was the last time you shagged somebody? A woman.

Rug Women are nothing but trouble, man. Give me a wank any day of the week.

Shuv Give yourself a wank you pervy cunt!

Rug Nah, but you ken what I mean.

Shuv (*laughs*) I ken.

Rug You ken?

Shuv Aye. Pure fucking hassle merchants. That's how I'm needing divorced, see?

Rug Should never've got hitched in the first place.

Shuv Aye well.

Rug Aye well?

Shuv I was young. My tadge was twitching. You ken what it's like at that age.

Rug What, you fucking past it now? (**Shuv** *mutters in disgust, shakes his head.*) 'Hold onto my zimmer while I get it in, hen.' Ha!

Shuv (*pause*) Anyhow, it's you who's fucking past it or something.

Rug Eh?

Shuv You're the one that's not up to the business, by Christ! Too much tugging, man, that's it: you've rubbed and rubbed till you've rubbed it away. 'Ta-ra! The amazing disappearing cock!'

Rug I'd give you a run for your money any day, you cunt.

Shuv Why all the worry then? (**Rug** *shrugs.*) You're feart she compares us! (*Pause.*) You sad wee fucker.

Rug   It's not that.

Shuv   Either that or you are an arse bandit.

Rug   Not that.

Shuv   What then?

Rug   Nothing.

Shuv   Come on you bastard.

Rug   Well . . .

Shuv   Fucking what!

Rug   She's a dog.

Shuv   Eh?

Rug   Lorraine, she's a fucking dog, she's bowfing. I wouldn't pish on her face if her mouth was on fire.

Shuv   (*pause*)   What did you say?

Rug   You're well shot of her, I tell you. All that yellow fat bulging through the fishnet tights . . .

Shuv   You! (*He jumps on* **Rug**, *wrestles him to the ground, rants.*) That's my wife you're fucking talking about!

Rug   What are you fucking doing?

Shuv   (*pinning him to the floor, knees on arms, leaning over his face*)   Don't you *ever* talk about Lorraine like that.

Rug   All right, man, all right. Get off my fucking arms, will you.

Shuv   I fucking . . . married her, right . . . and no cunt's going to . . . call her names . . . when I'm fucking breathing.

Rug   All right, all right, I'm sorry. (*They relax slightly.*) She is fucking mauchit but.

Shuv *slaps him on the face.* **Rug** *is shocked for a second then starts to struggle. He wiggles his shoulders and bucks his hips* *trying to get* **Shuv** *off. Eventually he makes a huge effort, and flings him away.* **Shuv** *tries to make it look like he's got off of his own accord, and steps away calmly.*

Shuv   You're a stupid cunt. That's your problem, Rug. Always has been. You have to ken when you're beaten, and you never do. And that's fatal, cause you're beaten most of the fucking time. (*Pause.*) You have to be able to admit it: 'Right, that's me fucked.' And then you can make a fresh start. Pick yourself up, start from the bottom, climb: you can only go up. (*Looks down at* **Rug** *lying on the floor.*) But see your problem, man: you never admit you're fucked, you're always floundering around down there in the shite and the pish and the puke, and you're grabbing folks' ankles shouting, 'Nothing wrong with me pal, I'm doing fine,' and then you get another boot in the teeth and you're down in the dirt again. (**Rug** *grunts.*) Stop flailing about man, stop shouting out: then get back on your own fucking feet.

Rug (*checking for broken bones, muttering*)   Cunt . . .

Shuv   What are you saying?

Rug (*struggling to sit up*)   Do you have to be so fucking rough all the time?

Rug *crawls to the front, collapses, moaning.* **Shuv** *looks down at him, smiling, almost laughs.*

Shuv   Come on pal, pull yourself together.

Rug (*rising up slightly, looking around*)   See's a drink then.

Shuv   Ah, you're a hardy bugger right enough. (**Rug** *collapses again.*)

Shuv *starts looking around, picks up various cans and bottles, shakes them. He finds a few dregs, drinks them himself.*

Shuv   Afraid you're out of luck, mate, nothing left at all.

Rug   Aw fuck.

Shuv I could get you a glass of water.

Rug (*sitting up*) Jesus, I'm not feeling that bad.

Both laugh. **Shuv** *takes out a comb and starts combing his hair.*

Rug What're you doing.

Shuv Raking.

Rug Oh. Why?

Shuv See my skull? It's a fucking fanny magnet.

Rug There's not much fucking fanny about here.

Shuv There will be at the party though.

Rug Oh, is there a party?

Shuv Too fucking right there is.

Rug Whereabouts?

Shuv I tellt you.

Rug No you never.

Shuv Aye I did. You've just forgotten. Jesus man, you're already a thick bastard, now don't go losing your memory as well.

Rug Well remind me then.

Shuv Oh, you coming are you?

Rug What? If you're going of course I'm fucking coming, you cunt!

Shuv You weren't invited.

Rug (*onto his feet*) Since when has that fucking mattered?

Shuv Ah well . . .

Rug Come on you cunt! I'm dying of thirst here, bored out of my skull – it's Friday night!

Shuv   And you're young, free and single – or if not free, then pretty fucking cheap.

Rug   Too fucking right man – two bottles of hootch and I'm anyone's!

Shuv   Right, smarten yourself up and we'll be off then.

Rug   Great (*Puts on jacket, shrugs: he's ready.*) So where is this party?

Shuv   Pilrig Street.

Rug   Who bides there?

Shuv   Fuck knows – I heard these two gadgies talking about it in the paki.

Rug   So nobody's actually asked you?

Shuv   Like you said, since when has that fucking mattered?

Rug   Suppose. (*He hacks, looks around, picks up a bottle and gobs into it, missing slightly.*) Gets a bit boring though. I mean, it'd be nice to be invited sometime, ken? Just once.

Shuv   We are invited!

Rug   Aye, we invited ourfuckingselves!

Shuv   If you're so worried about invites, how about us having a party? Just you and me. We could do it here: get some drink in, eh, a load of drink . . .

Rug   Dream on.

Shuv   How? It could be good. Get a bottle of Buckie, a few cans . . .

Rug   No fucking chance pal. Cause more than likely you'd get gatecrashers, mad cunts like us, coming in and trashing the place.

Shuv   That's true. And I just got it fixed how I like it.

(**Rug** *looks around at the dump.*) Right, I'll have a slash and then we'll nash, okay? (*He makes to leave, but* **Rug** *grabs his arm, excited.*)

Rug   Mind you though, Shuv, we could all chip in for a stripogram. Aye! The party's in full swing, then this bird in a raincoat comes in and starts doing a fucking strip! (*Jumping up onto the bed, seeing the strip.*) Jesus aye . . . big tits . . . fuck's sake! Right here on the bed. That close you could reach out and . . . anything, anything.

Shuv (*laughs at* **Rug**'s *pathetic dreams*)   Done it.

Rug   Eh?

Shuv   I had a stripogram back here once before.

Rug   Aye? When was that?

Shuv   Oh, six month ago.

Rug   I don't mind that, was it Hogmanay or something?

Shuv   Naw, it was just one Saturday there was fuck all going on. I was fed up with the boozer and I hadn't got my hole for a while. So I phoned up this agency, tellt them I had a stag night or something, and ordered this fucking French maid. Anyway, a couple hours later there's a knock on the door. 'Where's the party then?' she goes. 'The party's about to begin, darling. Just me and you, ken what I mean?' And guess what?

Rug   What?

Shuv   She buggers off! Away down the stair without so much as a flash of her gash!

Rug   Jesus Christ.

Shuv   Fucking atrocious, eh?

Rug   What, did you think she was going to strip off and let you poke her?

Shuv   Aye! These fucking stripogirls, man ... going round to somebody's house and doing the whole fucking raunchy routine: they're not exactly nuns, are they?

Rug (*pause*)   You can get them dressed as nuns though, eh?

Shuv (*pause*)   Aye. (*Both laugh. Then* **Shuv** *looks at* **Rug**, *and dives at him.*) Come on Mother Superior, show us your rosaries. (*They struggle on the bed for a few seconds.*)

Rug   Get off me, you tit.

Shuv   You love it.

Rug (*pushing* **Shuv** *away*)   Come on, let's get going if we're going.

Shuv   I tellt you, I'm needing a pish. (*Goes off to the lavvy.*)

Rug, *half lying on the bed, reaches out and switches on the cassette player. The last track on* Give Out But Don't Give Up *plays; it's not named, but the lyrics start: 'Life on your own don't really make you free.' It's a ballad;* **Rug** *gets up, dances around the room, a dreamy look in his eyes.* **Shuv** *comes back in at the start of the second verse. He watches* **Rug** *dancing. When the singer gets to 'Everybody needs somebody – I need you',* **Shuv** *strides over and smacks* **Rug** *hard in the mouth.* **Rug** *collapses. During the ensuing guitar solo, the music gets louder and louder, and* **Shuv** *puts the boot in to* **Rug**, *who crawls away behind the bed to escape.* **Shuv** *follows, still kicking. By the end of the solo, he tires of it, turns away, and switches off the screaming music. He sits on the bed, looking out front.*

Shuv   Oh aye, I forgot to tell you. Lorraine's going to the party too. They gadges I heard, they work with her out at Porty. (*Pause.*) Might be a good chance to get into her, eh? (**Rug** *crawls round from behind the bed, hauls himself up so he's leaning against it.*) What do you say, man?

Rug   Whatever you fucking want, pal. Do you want me to do Simone at the same time?

Shuv   You're sick you cunt. (*Pause.*) Anyway, she won't be there.

Rug   I was joking.

Shuv (*shaking his head*)   That's a sick joke, man.

Rug   Whatever you say.

Shuv (*jumping up*)   Well, come on, get your fucking arse into gear, are you coming or not?

Rug (*pause*)   I'm not coming.

Shuv (*pause*)   Well you're not staying here. This is my place.

Rug   I'm not staying here.

Shuv   Well if you're not staying here, and you're not coming out, what the fuck are you doing? I mean where the fuck are you going?

Rug   Nowhere.

Shuv   Nowhere?

Rug   Nowhere.

Shuv   Nah. That's where you are: nofuckingwhere. Here's where you're going: up my wife's hole.

Rug (*pause*)   Wherever. (*Getting to his feet.*)

Shuv   Too fucking right. (*He heads for the door.*) Come on, cunt.

Rug (*pause*)   Okay, prick.

Rug *switches on the tape machine. Primal Scream's 'Rocks' (same album) plays.* **Rug** *follows* **Shuv** *out the door. Lights fade.*

Blackden

a play in eight monologues

Characters

Brian Milne, *nineteen years old. A farm worker*
Shona Findlay, *twenty-two years old. Chef in the local pub*
Heather Roberts, *mid thirties. A council office worker*
Bill Murray, *forties. An auctioneer. Glaswegian by birth*

Blackden was first performed on 12 February 1997 at the Tron Theatre, Glasgow, by Castlemilk People's Theatre, with the following cast:

Brian Milne	Paul Mutch
Shona Findlay	Louise Ludgate
Heather Roberts	Jennifer Black
Bill Murray	Pat Welsh

Directed and designed by Peter Mackie Burns
Lighting by Stewart Steel

The characters sit among the audience till required on stage. The stage is bare.

Scene One
Isn't nature wonderful

Brian Milne *walks on. He is nineteen years old, works on his father's farm on the edge of the village. He wears standard non-work clothes: jeans, denim jacket. He is relaxed; he moves and talks easily, addressing the audience as if they were friends. His face is open and expressive, emotions showing clearly as they strike him. He looks around at the audience, gives them a smile, and starts talking.*

Brian Brian Milne. Nether Craigton. What like? The Milnes have aye bade here, Blackden. In fact, they've aye bade at Craigton. Going back (*Thinks.*) three hundred years or something. Patrick could tell you exactly, no doubt: he's up-to-date on all that history stuff. Up-to-date on the past, eh! But not me. I mean, most folk aren't, are they? (*Grins as a memory comes into his head.*) I mind the three of us sitting around talking about it a week or so ago – me, Paddy and Dek Duguid – and Dek was ranting on as usual about something at his college. (*Impersonates him and his rather aggressive speech.*) 'Ancient history, man. The prehistoric woodlands of Caledonia. What's that got to do with fuck all?' Excuse my French. Anyway, I goes, 'It'll be good when you finish though, eh Dek? I mean the pay with the forestry, you with your degree and that?' (*He's launched into the story now: we should see the three-way conversation in his movements.*)
'Aye,' he goes, 'but give me a chainsaw now and I'll cut their bastarding trees down. I don't need a college degree to do that!'
And then Paddy comes in with his smart-arse comments – cause he's *aye* got smart-arse comments. I mean I'm not slagging him, we go way back – born in Torphins maternity, half an hour apart! *But* . . . his arse is smart. (*Grins around, just to emphasise that this isn't a serious slag, then speeds on again.*) Anyway, Paddy goes, 'But you'll save a lot of energy with your education, Dek. Logic! Instead of

sawing the trees down, you can just argue with the
buggers, *persuade* them to lie down for you.'
'Never mind *trees*, Dek,' I goes, 'maybe you could
persuade some *woman* to lie down for you.' (*He laughs,
looks around to see if anyone else is joining in. Probably not: so
much the better.*) Aye, we all had a laugh at that.
(*Waves his hand: that's all that needs to be said about the friends.
The audience not laughing doesn't bother him: it just shows they're
not up to speed with his wit, yet.*) So that's me and Dek and
Paddy. The three fucketeers. Though Dek's been getting
a bit semi-detached, ken, since he's gone off to the
college. I mean, we still see him at weekends, and that,
he's still the same daft gype he always was. But he has
. . . changed. And that's something folk *just don't do* about
here. Change. Not much. (*Frowns, serious now, thinking; then
he pronounces:*)
Blackden. You're born into it, you work in it, you get
married in it . . . then you die in it. That's the way it's
always been. (*Shrugs: he's quite content with this.*) Fine. But
Dek's maybe . . . maybe starting to get ideas about . . .
well, who knows. (*Laughs as an idea occurs to him.*)
Marrying somebody from the college maybe! Aye, that'll
be it! Some tasty blonde from the city! Must be! (*Thinks.*)
That *must* be it. (*He grins, happy he's worked this out, then lets
his mind turn to Patrick, and his grin goes.*)
But it's not that with Paddy. I'd've kent if he had some
dame on the go. And he hasn't had since he had that
fling with Shona the chef. Christ, that was enough to
last him though! Warms her pants in the microwave
oven, that one! (*With great assurance:*) You ken these things
in a place like Blackden. There's no secrets here. That's
what Paddy always used to say, one of his sayings: 'No
secrets in Blackden. No secrets. Not a sausage.' (*Nods, in
complete agreement.*)
Like, say *I* was shagging . . . Marjorie Brindle, well,
aabody would ken about it. (*His face glows: she obviously
represents some peak of desirability.*) I'm not saying I *am*, like
– God's sake, she's only been here a week, give me a

chance! – but if I *was*, then aabody would ken about it.
Aabody but her man, of course.

Cause *one*, there's no such thing as a secret here. But
two, there are some things that everybody *makes on* are
secret. Like if I was shagging Marjorie B, everybody
would ken, and everybody would *also* ken that they
mustn't let on to her husband. (*Nods, glad that he's got this
point across, then looks around, sees some puzzlement.*)
Is that daft? I don't ken. But it works. In Blackden, at
least. Other places, right, a secret's something only one
person kens. Here, a secret is something that everybody
except one person kens. Get it? *The person it would hurt.*
(*Thinks a painful thought.*) Like, when Sprouty Hunter,
Paddy's father, when he had the cancer ... I think
everybody kent afore Paddy. Well, we didn't all ken for
sure, but we had a pretty good idea: you'd see him out
amongst his poly-tunnels, or carting his veg around in
the van ... and his skin was *grey*. He was thin as a
skeleton, with skeleton skin. *Scaly.* (*He shakes his head in
horror at the memory.*) But Paddy, well, I don't think he
ever noticed what was happening to his dad. I suppose
when you're biding with somebody, it all happens so
gradual that you miss it. Maybe the old man worsened a
little day by day, got a bit greyer and a bit greyer over
the months, and Paddy didn't catch on to what was
happening, just didn't notice. Till the very end. Then he
caught on in a big way. (*Looks down.*) Aye, he took it bad
when his old man died. This time last year, it was. All
of a sudden. Sprouty'd lain there for ever, just inching
more and more into greyness, then suddenly – (*Claps.*) –
he's gone.

Paddy took it real bad. I'll tell you how bad he took it:
he never came to the pub for *two weeks*. (*Pause. Shakes his
head.*) Aye. But at the funeral he never grat. He just
looked around, *watched* everybody. You'd've thought he
was coping fine. But then he disappears for two weeks!
(*Walks around in a small circle: five steps or so.*) Aye, when I
say disappear, I don't mean like now. Cause we all kent

where he was then: up at his house. I ken he's not there
this time, cause I was there yesterday, looking for him.
(*He walks around in the circle again. When he faces out front
again he's thought of something funny.*) He never grat when
his dad died, but you should've heard him when his
bloody bike disappeared, after the roup on Saturday!
End of world civilisation, that was. You'd've thought
he'd lost his trusty pizzle, never mind a rusty old pusher.
It was an antique, it really was, belonged to his grandad
or something. Muckle iron thing, weighed half a ton,
basket big enough for a sack of tatties over the front
wheel. Grandad used to do deliveries for the market
garden with it, afore they got the van. And now here's
Paddy, heaving all over the countryside on the damn
thing: to work, to the pub, to dances even. (*Imitates
Patrick, leaning casually against the dance-hall door:*) 'Can I
give you a hurl home, Angie?' (*Girl's seductive voice:*) 'Oh
aye, Patrick, have you got reclining seats?' 'No, but I've
got a basket over the front wheel: you sit there and I'll
crank away!'
(*Shakes his head.*) What a man. (*Wanting to communicate
something about Patrick's character – something admirable, or at
least memorable.*) He aye does things his own way, that's
for sure. You can't force Paddy into anything, you just
have to let him think it through and come up with *his*
way.
Of course, sometimes that can have its drawbacks too:
thinking ower much, instead of just going with the flow.
I was saying that to him on Saturday night, at the stovie
dance. Here's me, giving it laldie up on the dance floor
(*Starting here, and for the next few lines, he disco dances around
the floor, his comments always directed to where he's imagining
Patrick sitting.*) and the whole damn time Paddy's sitting
over at the side, glumshing into his pint. I go up to
him, right, and I say, 'Come on man, go with the flow:
get up there and dance, stop thinking about it.'
And he's like, 'I ken, I ken: just take the fucking plunge.
(*Pause while Patrick thinks. As he's about to start dancing, he*

hesitates again.) Not consider the ifs and buts, (*Another pause for thought, another hesitation.*) forget the pros and cons, just do it. That's my problem Bri,' he goes, (*Long pause, final half-hearted attempt to dance, immediately abandoned.*) 'I think about it all too much.'

'You do, Paddy,' I said, 'but you're wanting to get your hole, right, not a fucking Higher, so switch your brain off for an hour, and let your balls do the thinking.' (*He hip-thrusts away across the floor, some woman in his sights, the conversation wrapped up good and proper.*)

(*Stops dancing, shrugs, back in the present.*) It works for me, anyway. I mean sometimes you get knocked back, but . . . (*Shrugs, indicating he's not worried.*) Here's my theory about it: if sex had anything to do with brains . . . *how the hell are rabbits so good at it?* Eh? Ha! Stupid wee shites: brain the size of a carrot. Not me: *cock* the size of a carrot, me! (*Laughs.*) Aye, a big carrot, like. (*Thinks.*) Course, it's not really that shape. Well . . . aye. And the colour's wrong too. (*Thinks of something else, laughs again.*) Here, listen, you'll like this. Seeing as we're on the subject of rodents. (*Looking over his shoulder, as if the folk concerned might walk in and overhear at any minute.*) Marjorie Brindle, right – she knocked me back! – her and her man . . . (*Frowns: doesn't know the name.*) . . . the mannie Brindle, they were to be staying up at the Sangsters' B&B at Braeheid. Till this croft they've bought got done up. (*Rolls his eyes.*) Goodman's Croft! I ask you: doing up that old rickle of stones! They could've got one of those Norwegian wooden houses in a kit for half the price: triple glazing, underfloor heating, the lot. Christ, I'd've put it up for them! Just like stickle-bricks, those things! Anyway, they drove up to the Sangsters' last Sunday night: Cherokee jeep, of course. Ken what happens Monday morning? They're sitting at the breakfast table tucking into their bacon and eggs – 'Yum yum, very nice Mrs Sangster: and you say you laid these eggs yourself?' – when there's a scratching at the kitchen window. They look up, and there's a fucking *rat* sitting

there, raking its paws down the glass! Great big greasy
thing. Jean Sangster shrieks – 'Eeeergh!' – and waves
her *People's Friend* at the beast. The Mannie Brindle goes,
'Another egg coming, Mrs Sangster?', and Marjorie goes,
(*With an ecstatic sigh.*) 'Isn't nature wonderful!'
(*He hoots with laughter.*) Can you believe it? But that's not
all. (*Rat mime.*) Scratch, scratch ... Marjorie's wittering
on about how she's going to save some of her toast and
go out and feed the fucking thing, and does Mrs
Sangster think it would like a bit of marmalade ...
when, KABOOM! Willie Sangster's got his twelve-bore
out and the rattan's splattered all over the yard ...
blood and guts on the window pane ... dribble dribble.
(*Laughs, shakes his head.*) Willie walks in, quite the thing,
sits down and starts drinking his tea.
'You shot that ... little animal,' says Marjorie. (*Almost in
tears.*) 'That's *terrible.*'
'I ken,' says Willie. 'It is a terrible waste of shot.' Slurp
slurp. 'Ken what the latest way to get rid of the bastards
is? Saucers of Coca Cola down in the barn. Saucers of
Coke. The buggers smell the sweetness, come out at
night and drink it all. What they don't ken is this: rats'
guts can't digest the carbon dioxide. Can't deal with it
at all, can't even fart it out.' (The mannie Brindle
chokes on his toast.) 'So what happens is, they drink and
drink, and they bloat away out. They puff up like
balloons, so fat they can't get back in their hidey holes:
furry balloons with rat tails, scuttling about the floor.
Next day you just go around the barn with a pointed
stick, and pop! pop! pop!' (*Mimes rat guts exploding
everywhere.*)
At this the mannie Brindle jumps up, dashes out the
door, and bleahhh! (*Throws up.*) Giving the vermin a feed
after all. Marjorie's made of stronger stuff. She's like,
'That poor wee defenceless beastie. I thought country
people were meant to be *at one* with nature.'
Willie looks at her. 'It was a mercy killing,' he says.
'*What?* That was cold-blooded *murder*, Mr Sangster.'

'Nah nah,' says Willie, 'shooting was merciful right
enough: how do *you* fancy being popped with a pointed
stick? (*Jabs at her.*) Thrrrrruuuuuuppppp.' (*The noise and
action of a loosed balloon whizzing round the room.*)
(*After he's finished laughing.*) And *that* is why the Brindles
moved out of Braeheid and into the Ould Mill Inn. I
heard it myself from Willie. There's no secrets in
Blackden, right enough! 'Isn't nature wonderful'!

A few seconds more laughing, then he walks off.

Scene Two
While I'm alive I intend to live

Shona Findlay *walks on, rather hesitantly: a mixture of
reluctance and defiance. She is twenty-two and is dressed in her
work clothes: chef's white jacket, slightly grubby, and checked
trousers. A cloth hangs from a loop at her waist. Her hair is
either very short, or is pinned back tightly; no make-up. She looks
at the audience less openly than Brian: it seems she doesn't really
want to be here, and doesn't take too much pleasure in the
situation. She relaxes very slightly as she talks, but even then she is
still noticeably nervous or reluctant. Her sentences tend to be short
and jabby; her eyes flit around and don't make contact with
anybody for more than half a second; her body language appears
defensive much of the time: folded arms, shrugs, head-shakes.*

Shona Shona Findlay. The Caravan, Corse Woods.
But . . . (*Pause.*) I don't . . . I don't ken him really. Well,
I ken who he *is*, like. Fuck's sake: round here you ken
who aabody is – aye, and every bastard kens you! And
it's true I was speaking to him on Friday, just. But – it's
not like I chum around with him or anything. It's not
like, ken, anything was *happening* between us. It's his
sister I'm friendly with, really: Helen. (*Shrugs.*) Well, even
there you see: I haven't heard from *her* for ages either.
This time last year since I saw her. She went away to
uni, see, and that . . . pissed me off. (*A nervous laugh.*) I

ken it's daft now, but – I was just a bairn then. I mean,
this was . . . three year ago. There we was, best pals, me
and Helen, and suddenly she announces she's off to uni
in Edinburgh. I mean to say, can you just abandon your
pals like that? Follow your own. . . ? Ach, forget it. (*She
turns away from the audience, stares off to the side for a moment.
Then she turns back to the front, as if giving in to the fact that
more is required.*)

Everything changes, eh? Six month later *I* fucked off
too. But only as far as Aberdeen: out to Altens, ken,
cooking for the oil men. Pretty good set up, actually,
cause they paid me to go to the college andall. Which
meant when the contract ended I could come back to
Blackden and get the job at the Old Mill.

(*Shakes her head.*) A chef at the Old Mill Inn! If you'd told
me that when I was a lassie drinking here I'd've laughed
in your face. Mince pies and bridies out of the heat box
on top of the bar, that was your lot back then. Now?
Cordon fucking bleu, take it or leave it, mate. I'll say
this about John Wilson: he's definitely put the place up-
market, ken. He may be a foul-mouthed bad-tempered
penny-gripping shite, but he's put the Mill (*Points.*) up-
market. The last owners didn't even ken there was a
market! (*Shrugs.*) Like I say, everything changes. You
might not like it, but it's true.

Anyway. Patrick Hunter. Paddy. He comes into the
kitchen on Friday night, and I'm up to my fucking eyes
in it. Tenderising steaks I was, getting cheapskate
Wilson's cheap cuts ready for steak and stout pies on
Saturday. (*Acts it out.*) You get your steak, right, you get
your mallet and WHUMP, WHUMP, flip it over,
WHUMP, WHUMP . . . chuck it on the tray. (*She is
relaxing slightly now, as if the routine action reduces her self-
consciousness.*) Next one: WHUMP, WHUMP . . . Then
somebody walks in. 'What is it *now*?' But when I look
up, it's not Wilson down with another order, it's . . .
somebody I didn't expect, takes me a second to click . . .
ah! Patrick! Helen's wee brother. No so wee now, of

course: eighteen, nineteen, something like that. Anyway,
I'm like, (*Back to the energetic mime.*) 'Fuck's sake pal, what
you fucking gowking at?' WHUMP! Cause I was in a
right foul mood that night (you maybe guessed).
WHUMP! And he blabs on about something, no having
seen me for a while, and how I'm looking good, and
I'm like . . . *yeah, so?* So I say, WHUMP, 'Fuck's sake
Paddy, can you no tell I'm up to my eyes here? Drew
the dishwasher's off sick,' WHUMP, 'so I'm having to
do that as well as all the fucking cooking. And as if *that*
wasn't bad enough, John Wilson's gone and said he'll
make the stovies for the dance in the hall thenight.'
WHUMP! 'Stovies for a hundred and twenty fucking
folk! Aye, he said *he'd* do them, what he really meant
was, "I'll tell that dumb skivvy Shona Findlay to do
them" – as well as every other fucking job in this
minuscule fucking antiques roadshow of a kitchen.'
WHUMP!!! (*Pause. She wipes sweat from her forehead.*)
'You'd think with all the siller he spent upstairs,' says
Paddy, peering about, 'he could've fitted out the kitchens
as well.'
But I explained: Wilson's all fucking show. (*Obviously a
favourite gripe.*) The punters don't see down here, so it
doesn't fucking matter. Behind the fancy decor it's the
same old shite: non-stop slaving for the likes of me.
WHUMP!
'So, Shona,' he says after a while, 'are you coming to
the Young Farmers' hooley, then?'
What's this? I think to myself. Has he come in here to
ask me for a *dance*? So I go, 'Well, I'll be over with the
stovies, that's for sure. Steaming cauldrons of grease, ten
o'clock delivery!' And he grins, this big grin on his face.
I'm beginning to think, has he got the hots for me or
something? Eh? (*Laughs.*) I mean, not that he's not a fine
enough loon. He is. Not bad looking or nothing. But he
seems *young*, ken – (*Shrugs.*) maybe just cause I think of
him as Helen's wee brother. (*Pause.*) Anyway, I wasn't
really thinking all this through, I was just, like, playing

along, going, 'Okay Paddy, I'll see you there.' (*Shimmies her hips.*) 'Save the last dance for me, eh?' (*Pause. Changes back to her usual dourness.*) But I was only kidding, ken. (*Pause.*) Surely he wouldn't've thought I was serious? I mean . . . I hardly ken him at all. Ask Bobby Bastard. Ask anyone.

Anyway. (*She pats her jacket pockets, then her trouser pockets, looking for her fags. They're not there.*) There you go. (*She gazes offstage for a moment, then back to the front once more.*) Aye. He wants a pie for his granny and grandad: that's why he's under my feet. (*Frowns.*) Or is it just an excuse? (*Thinks.*) No, he really does. He's meant to take them their tea and he's forgot it, wants to get a pie from me. Here's something about the Hunters: they're real good with the old folks. Helen was always like that, blethered away to all the old mannies and wifies. No me! Jesus Christ, I just get bored with the bastards. (*Looks around, nervously, then spits it out.*) Euthanasia? I'm all for it. *Compulsory* for aabody over the age of fucking sixty: WHUMP! 'You're euthanasiaised!' Ha. (*Looks around to see how folk have reacted. Shrugs.*) Anyway, Paddy's the same as his sister, it seems. And especially since . . . their father died. That was a year ago now. More or less exact; Mhairi up in the bar was reminding me, cause I was still living in town then. (*Pause.*) Seems he spends a lot of time with the old folks these days. Suppose he's worried about them going next.

(*A thought comes into her head, and for the first time she's positively passionate about something, even if it is a fairly negative notion. She tries to make eye contact now.*) This is what I *mean*: you never ken when it's going to happen. I mind saying this to Paddy once: you get folk living their whole lives, so scared of *dying*, that they never fucking get a *life*! To hell with that! If you kent for certain you were going to get tenderised at the age of sixty – (*Mimes a hammer blow to her head.*) WHUMP! – well, you'd stop worrying about it, that's my theory. You'd ken how long you'd got, and you'd make the most of it. (*Suddenly she stops, as if realising*

she's given a bit too much of herself away.) That's what I
reckon, anyway. You'll probably think it's shite. (*Shrugs.*)
I don't care. It's how I live my life: while I'm alive I
intend to fucking *live*! (*Pause, during which she looks around
defiantly. After a couple of seconds, an ironic look comes across her
face.*)
As far as you *can* live in this place. I mean, it's not
exactly . . . I don't know, *Ibiza*, is it? It's not New York.
It's not even Aberfuckingdeen. Don't get me wrong, you
can *exist* here: you can get work, you can have your
mates, you can drink, shag, dance the Gay Gordons to
your heart's content. You can even get a house to live
in if you're lucky and there's not some oil man cruising
by at that minute with more siller than sense. Aye aye
aye: you can *exist* in Blackden. But is that the same as
living? (*Shrugs: but it's a different shrug from a couple of minutes
ago. It's less a dismissal now, more a genuine admission of doubt:
she is relaxing slightly.*) A couple year ago I'd've said no, I
would've been *out* of here, off to the bright lights. Hih, I
was out of here! Like I said: working at Altens, going to
the parties, the raves . . . But I don't ken: you get fed
up of all that after a while. Well, I did anyway. You
kind of get to thinking about your old pals back home:
what're they up to, what's the gossip, what's going on.
So you come back and . . . fuck all's going on! (*Laughs.*)
Aye, the grass is always greener in the next park along.
Christ, that makes us all sound like cows! (*Shakes her head,
laughs again.*) Mind you, it seems to me most folk are like
bloody cattle. (*She looks offstage again, briefly, then out front,
speaks bitterly.*) They stand about like dumb heifers, eating
their grass and getting fatter and mounting each other
and getting fatter. Till one day a big transporter comes
to take them away. 'At last,' they think as they drive
through the slaughterhouse gates, 'at last something
interesting is going to happen!' (*She feels she's exposing
herself now, and might as well plunge on. She walks about
nervously, and speaks her final lines with more energy than
anything previously.*)

Change, change, change, that's what it's all about:
you've got to keep changing, to give yourself the illusion
that your life's fucking interesting. Constant novelty,
that's the thing, to distract you from the fact that you're
basically chewing the cud for seventy years. (*Shrugs.*)
Maybe Paddy's just fancied a change, just went for it.
Like I say, I hardly ken him, but that would be my
guess . . . *whoever* it was had gone off I'd guess: they just
fancied a change. (*Pause.*) I ken I do.

Scene Three
I never stopped to listen to the feelings

Heather Roberts *walks on, looks around the stage. She is
the younger sister of Paddy's mother, and works in the council
office in the nearest town. She is in her mid thirties, wears casual
but stylish clothes: just a little bit arty. She's confident and calm,
or at least appears so most of the time. She takes a couple of steps
on, looks around, then goes off again. She reappears with a chair.
She sets this stage front centre, facing straight out. Then she
considers, and moves it back a bit, angles it slightly. All this is
done not neurotically, or fussily, but just as if she's used to having
things arranged precisely and nicely. She sits down, and
immediately takes out cigarettes and a lighter; she lights one, and
takes a long deep draw. She smokes more or less constantly
throughout the following. She doesn't exactly ignore the audience,
but neither does she really engage with them at first: she's a little
too poised, too in control. Her voice is soft and level; to begin with
it sounds almost as if she's thinking aloud.*

Heather   I blame myself. To an extent. Not that I
think I drove him away in any sense. No, it was . . . a
whole lot of factors that contributed to that. But I blame
myself for not noticing he was on the verge of it. (*Pause.*)
Not noticing! Dear oh dear: I didn't have to notice, I
just had to listen. But of course I was too busy *talking* to
listen. As per always, as Patrick would say.

(*Takes a drag, looks up.*) Sorry. Heather Roberts. Pond Cottage, up by the big house.

(*Another drag, then she begins.*) I took a run up to The Strath on Friday night, and he was just away to go out, so I didn't stay long. Moira – that's my sister, his mother – she was away to Edinburgh, a long weekend, visiting Helen at the uni. And just getting away from this place: this time of year's difficult for her.

So. I didn't stay: I gave him a lift down the road in fact. (*Thinks. Impersonates Paddy, jumping up with his excitement and irritation.*) 'I'm fed up of getting lifts here, there and everywhere – everybody jumping down my throat to give me lifts every minute of the day.' This is Patrick, by the way. 'I'm completely *scunnered* with it, Heather! I want to get somewhere under my *own* steam for a change!' (*She sits down again, smiles briefly.*) But that was later, that was . . . four o'clock on Sunday morning for God's sake! (*Frowns.*) When he told me his . . . story. (*Almost resentful.*) When he put it off of his shoulders and onto mine. (*Sinks down, as if a weight has been laid on her, then shakes her head to clear this thought away.*) Scrub that. But on Friday night he seemed happy enough with getting a lift down to the pub. (*Thinks back, and laughs, genuine warmth obvious now.*) He was blethering away as usual. He doesn't half come out with some daft stuff! What was it he was on about? Oh aye: the names of Scottish rivers, of all things. Apparently Helen has a friend in the States who bides by a river called the Cranberry River. Patrick thought this was *brilliant*. He reckoned you could just dive in and drink the whole thing with a name like that on it. 'But what've we got here?' he goes. 'At the back of Bennachie there's the Gadie – gads! And the Spey: spaying's something nasty you do to a cat. And the *Bogie*! Christ, Scotland, you have to be joking: the river o Bogie!'

(*Takes a drag for punctuation.*) So of course me, *I* rise to this, 'Oh, you're not a nationalist then, Patrick?' And he goes, 'No, Aquarius.'

Which just gets me going, ken, sets me off on this big
political speech. Cause it's in a *mess* this bit of the
country. It may look bonny with the hills and the
heather and all that, but it's a bloody mess,
economically. Subsidies and overdrafts, that's what this
place runs on. And here's a young guy – articulate,
intelligent, born and bred here, the kind of guy that
should *care* about these things – and he's joking about it
– and telling me he didn't vote at the election! (*Shakes
her head.*) Dear oh dear. (*The following is what she said to
Paddy, but it's addressed now to the audience.*)
'What about your pals that don't have jobs? Look at
public transport since privatisation – that affects you –
one bus a *day* into town? Pathetic!' (*This to the audience.*)
Aye, and none on a Sunday, so wherever he is, he's not
got there by bus! 'And what about folk in the village,' I
says, 'native Blackdenners, that can't get a home?
Richard and Isobel Marshall: two years married and still
biding with her folks, cause they can't afford a house,
cause they're all bought at great high prices by incomers
to the village – incomers to the country! The National
Party stands up for the people of Blackden, FOR THE
PEOPLE OF SCOTLAND!'
(*Realises she's getting too strident. Shuts up, sits back, lights
another fag maybe.*) And Patrick says, 'Aye, and you stand
up for the Queen as well.' (*A chuckle.*) Which is funny.
But it's also avoiding the serious point by making a joke
of it. (*Pause.*) Why do folk do that? Is it a Scottish thing?
We'll make a million jokes about the English being
toffee-nosed tosspots with funny accents, but we won't
lift a hand to get them out of the country – not even by
putting a cross on a piece of paper.
So you get the tragic situation where Billy Connolly's a
national hero and John Maclean's all but forgotten.
(*Pause.*)
Anyway, we're driving down the hill from The Strath,
chugging along in the old Beetle, and I kind of wave
out the window at the countryside and the lights of the

village down in the den below. I try a different line of
attack. 'Don't you like this part of the world you're
living in?' I say to him.

'I like it fine,' says Patrick. 'This part of the world? I
love it! I'd like to *marry* it!'

That was one of his phrases. God knows where it came
from, but they used to say it all the time, the kids.
Helen would ask Patrick if he liked ice cream, and when
he said aye she'd go, 'Why don't you *marry* it then?'
(*Smiles.*) One time, when Patrick was about seven, we
were all out for a picnic, up Ben Macdeamhain, and
Moira and Alec – Sprouty, everybody called him, cause
of the gardening – they must've been cuddling in the
heather. Cause Patrick goes up to them and says,
'Mummy, do you like Daddy?' And Moira said of course
she liked him, and Patrick said, 'Well, why don't you
marry him then?' (*Laughs.*)

He was always saying stuff like that as a kid, always
happy. Always went his own way, never listened to a
word anybody said. Always coming up with daft ideas
from God knows where.

He hasn't changed! Like this new theory: places are
great till you put a name to them. Names ruin it all.
Cause once you name a place, you fence it off from the
rest of the earth's surface, and then you start having to
like it more than *other* bits of the earth, that happen to
have different names. (*She imitates Patrick getting excited.*)
'Kincardine O' Corse? A townful of tinks! Kemnay?
They beat us at football! (*Jumping up.*) Let's all go over
in a couple cars and duff them up: Blackden Boot Boys
versus Kemnay Casuals! DEATH TO KEMNAY!'
'Patrick . . .' I says.

'In fact, why stop there. As soon as you put words to
anything you get in a fankle. Death and life: all part of
the same thing till we pin two words on it and split it in
two and get hung up on one of them. Good and bad,
right and wrong: where does one end and the other
begin? Nobody knows for sure, cause they're all joined

together once you get away from the words. You *can't*
split right from wrong!' (*Pause, to let Paddy's shouts fade out.*)
Okay, it's obvious now: I should've worked out he was
pretty damn upset about something. I mean, does that
sound like normal to you? Like sensible?

It's clever – he *is* clever, could've gone to uni like his
sister if he hadn't missed so much school in his fifth year
and messed up his exams. Aye, it's clever, but is it
sensible?

(*Shakes her head.*) He was upset, upset. But I honestly
thought he was just arguing. At the time I thought it
was *ideas* he was coming out with. I never stopped to
listen to the *feelings*. (*She sits down again, not quite so poised
as before: she's concentrating on what she's thinking now rather
than how she's holding herself.*)

So I says, 'Okay Patrick, you're not patriotic, you're not
a nationalist. Okay. It's a principle you've got there, and
you're sticking to it. Fine. But the problem with
principles is, while you're so busy holding onto them,
you haven't a free hand to help anyone else. And folk
need help, Patrick. They do.'

'It's not a principle,' he says after a minute. 'It's just . . .
I don't know what it is. A feeling.'

A feeling. (*Nods, sad.*) He actually said it, now I come to
think of it. Christ, he must've been bad: it takes a *hell* of
a crisis to get a Scottish man talking about feelings.
(*Thinks for a minute, then gets up and walks away, smoking hard.
After a few seconds she stops and speaks loudly, very emotional.*)
It's not just men. It's everybody in this dreich bloody
down-trodden country! We all keep them shut away, like
they're top secret or something! Like they'd shrivel up
and die if they ever saw daylight!

Course, it's partly having somebody to tell them to. I
mind Patrick saying that, one of his sayings: 'There's no
secrets in Blackden, no secrets . . . just no one listening.'
And he's right. What about me, for instance? Who
could I talk to about my feelings when Roberts
buggered off? Well, okay, Moira was there. (*Pause.*) But

what *about* Moira? Her man dies of cancer at the age of forty-five. Who's going to listen to how she feels? Watching him lying there for weeks, for months! Who can she talk to? Helen didn't come home till the very end: there was only Patrick, for months ... I don't ken how she could stand it, I'd've, I'd've ... (*Stops talking for a moment, bites her lip.*) I don't know what I'd've done. You never know till you've been in that situation. You never know till you've sat by that bed, and watched ... someone you love ... (*Shakes her head, looks down, upset.*) I understand why folks give up on feelings. Maybe it's not so daft. They're too damn painful! Logic, that's what I'm going in for now. A cold, clear look at the world. Aye. It all comes down to economics anyway. Feelings are banned. Cause ... the stronger the feeling ... the more it hurts you when it fucks up. And it always fucks up.

Do you like him? Aye! Why don't you *marry* him, then? Do you *really really* like him? *Aye!* Why don't you *kill* him then.

Christ. Where is he?

She walks around for a moment, worrying, trying to calm down, doesn't succeed, and walks off.

Scene Four
Work, a wife, responsibilities, habits

Bill Murray *the auctioneer walks on, carrying a wooden box under one arm: his kist. He is forty or a little older, heavily built, red in the face from a lot of outdoor work and a lot of whisky. He wears a farmer's tweed jacket and bunnet. He walks rather stiffly to the front, looks out around the audience, sizing them up like a seasoned performer (which he is). Then he sets down the kist and adjusts its position with the toe of his boot. He goes to step up on it, then changes his mind, turns his back on the audience and takes a quick swig from a hip flask which he then slips back inside his jacket. He introduces himself.*

Bill   Bill Murray, Murray Marts. Roups, cattle auctions, displenish sales; furniture, livestock, second-hand motors; antique valuation; houses cleared: your place or mine.

He looks around, beaming, then steps up on his kist and gets going – loudly, confidently, cheerily.

What am I bid for the tale of Patrick Hunter? Chance of a bargain here, chance of a bargain, the full set: blood sweat *and* tears, yes folks all human life is there, so who'll start the bidding, who'll start the bidding . . . at five pounds . . . ? (*So far he's been relatively measured: now he starts rattling the words off in true auctioneer style.*) . . . five pounds five pounds who'll bid five I'm bid five at the back five at the back and *six* and seven and eight bid eight bid I'm bid eight at the front sir and TEN POUNDS with you madam that's up to ten for Patrick Hunter, I'm bid twelve bid twelve, I'm bid fourteen, I'm bid fourteen, fifteen bid fifteen bid – BLOOD SWEAT AND TEARS, LET'S *HAVE* YOU! – sixteen bid, at the front sixteen pounds, and (*His eyes and hands switching back and forth between the bidders.*) seventeen, nineteen pounds, and twenty? Twenty? TWENTY-FIVE pounds to the lady at the back, are we all in at twenty-five bid all in at twenty-five, twenty-five pounds I'm bid twenty-five, twenty-five pounds for Patrick Hunter? Hammer's up at twenty-five . . . Thank you! (*He stomps his heel on the top of the box, the sound marking the closing of the sale. Then, grinning around at everybody, he takes out the hip-flask, salutes the buyer with it.*)

Good bid madam, very good bid. (*He drinks.*) Slinging in the extra fiver like that: good move. Seems a lot, does it not, a jump of a fiver, and everybody else thinks, 'Glory be, this is a woman with money!' But it's only a fiver, and what's that these days? Bugger all! A fiver? You can hardly get a half-bottle for a fiver! So . . . (*Another salute, another drink, then he gets down off the kist, paces around a little.*) You'll be wanting your story then? Cause it's just the story you get, mind, not the lad himself! (*Laughs.*) Oh

aye, that *would* be a bargain! Twenty-five pound for a
day's work – well, maybe – but look at this. (*Checks his
watch, taps the face of it.*) We're into overtime now, see:
time and a half once you get to this time of night. Does
that spoil your plans? (*Laughs.*) Ach, I'm only kidding.
For he's not here anyway. Like I said: it's just the story
you get, not the lad himself. Cause nobody knows where
the lad himself is! (*Sits down on his kist, looking serious now.*)
He didn't turn up for his work today. Nine o'clock, no
Patrick. Funny, he's usually always on time. Nine *thirty*,
no Patrick. He's never been this late! Ten o'clock, still
no bloody Patrick. And I'm thinking, 'Where the hell's
that boy?' He's never been off sick before, but it's
possible. So I phone his house: no reply. I'm racking my
brains ... till I mind on what happened on Saturday at
the roup at Goodman's Croft. (*Notices/remembers that the
audience don't know what this is, so goes off on a tangent
explaining.*)
Goodman's? You've never *seen* such a pile of shite!
Listen, I've been in this job for more than twenty year
now, ever since I came up here. Believe me, I've seen
some run-down dilapidated dumps of farms in my time.
But Goodman's was the worst! Folk here think the cities
are full of slums: I'll tell you, they've got nothing on the
country round Blackden! Up to your arse in mud and
shite, rats running all over, sheep shaggers in the byre
and New Age bastards shitting at the stone circle.
(*Laughs.*) Christ, I love the country life. But Goodman's
was bad even for here. Talk about the Dark Ages.
Machinery solid with rust, wrecks of old threshing mills
and reapers – and a Fordson tractor I bet he'd had
since he first got rid of his pair o horse! (*Laughs.*) I'll tell
you how ancient the Fordie was: it was bought by an
antique collector from Elgin. He's going to restore it and
show it at the traction engine rally! (*Laughs.*) And it's
only a couple weeks since Dod o Goodman's was out
ploughing the parks in it!
(*Up to another level of storytelling.*) Oh aye, the Fordies are

great. They built them to last in the old days, did they
not? Oh aye, great wee machines. Hell, I know for a
fact that Dod's been as far as *London* in his! Aye! I mind
the time *fine.* (*Looks around to check that the audience is
listening: adjusts his approach accordingly.*) Two or three year
ago now, I saw Dod o Goodman's go puttering through
the village, a miserable look on his face. So I waves to
him, and he stops. 'What's up Dod?' I says.

And he goes, (*Impersonation.*) 'I've sellt some neeps' – he
had a right girny voice – 'I've sellt a cartload of neeps
to a chiel in London, but he wants me to deliver them,
and I don't ken where it is.'

'London?' I say. 'You better head south, Dod.'

So he climbs back into his Fordie and heads off down
the road, bogey behind him spilling neeps every bump
he goes over. Well, after a while, he comes to a town.
'Is this London?' he calls out to a woman in the street.
'Michty no, man,' she replies, 'this is Fettercairn, you've
a way to go yet.'

So Dod nods and waves and heads off south again, and
after a long while he comes to a great big city. 'Aye
aye,' he thinks, and he asks a boy standing on a street
corner, 'Is this London?'

The boy looks at him like he's daft. 'Hell no,' he says,
'this is Glasgow, fair on south!'

So Dod frowns and drives on. 'Govey dick,' he thinks,
'it's a hell of a long road away from Blackden, this
London place . . .' *Eventually* he comes to this enormous
big town, he can't see the end of it even. And sure
enough, there's a sign at the side of the road: CITY OF
LONDON. 'About time!' he thinks, and pulls over. There's
a guy walking down the pavement, bowler hat and
briefcase, and Goodman's shouts at him, 'This is
London, is it not?'

The lad looks back. 'Of course it is,' he says.

'Well then,' says Dod, 'where do you want your neeps?'
(*He laughs uproariously, wipes his brow, takes another drink. Then
he walks about a bit, laughing to himself, looking out at the*

audience to see if they enjoyed his story.)

Now. Here's a funny thing. I was telling this story to
Patrick on Saturday there. And the wife as well, Sandra.
Fly time it was, and we were all having a cup of tea –
or something *(He raises the flask.)* – and Ronaldson from
Howbrae was yapping on as always. *(Shakes his head,
suddenly bitter.)* That bald rusty-headed bastard can't half
yap, I tell you: talk the gold horns off a brass billy-goat,
Ronaldson. And all of it shite!

Anyway, here's me telling all about old Dod driving
down to London, and there's Patrick standing soaking it
all in. *(Nods at the obvious significance of this.)* Know what I
think? I think he's buggered off there himself! Aye! Just
like that! I mean . . . he could at least've let me know
he wasn't coming into work. I was worried! I'll tell you
how worried I was: I even phoned the polis up at
Mortlich, told them I wanted to report a missing person.
'How long's he been missing?' they said. 'Twenty-four
hours,' I said. 'That's not missing,' they go, 'that's just
late.' I tried to tell them that Patrick was a real good
worker, he'd never been late in all the four months he'd
been with the Mart. But they weren't interested. No
crime had been committed, so they couldn't do f-all.
'He'll turn up,' they said. 'But let us know if you find a
body.' And he laughed, like that was *funny.*

Nah, nobody's murdered Patrick: everybody liked him.
And who'd kidnap him? The Blackden branch of the
mafia? Nah. The truth is, I've no idea where he's gone.
Christ, I shouldn't have to worry about this. I'm just the
one that pays his wages, nothing more.

(Shakes his head, considering the future with an absent apprentice.)

Aye, wherever he's gone, I'm afraid he's blotted his copy
book this time. Just taking off like that. *(Drinks: he's
definitely getting a bit redder in the face, and a bit looser in his
movements as the whisky goes down. His sternness changes back to
warmth almost immediately.)* It's a shame, cause he's got the
makings of a good auctioneer that lad. The gift of the
gab, that's what he's got, and you need that. You need

other talents as well, like, but the first of all is: you need
to be able to talk and think at the same time. Oh aye.
(*Catching somebody's sceptical eye.*) It's not as easy as you
think, that; you should try it sometime. Auctioneers and
politicians, they're the two lots of folk that're best at it.
You see them on telly all the time, aye, the politicians:
somebody asks them a difficult question and, 'Blah blah
blah blah blah blah blah . . .' off they go, nineteen to
the dozen, and they don't have a bloody *clue* where
they're headed. They're just making it up as they go
along!

Anyway, Patrick's good at that. In my opinion. My
expert opinion. You should hear him, blethering away at
some bit of nonsense or other: he just *launches* into it,
doesn't know where he's headed at all, just makes it up
as he goes along. Aye, and now I come to think of it, I
bet he's headed off like that too. (*Considers, nods.*)

Aye, forget London. He's not delivering a cartload of
neeps to London. Here's what he's gone and done,
Patrick. 'I'm fed up with this place,' he's said to himself.
'I'm getting out of here.' And *off* he *went*. (*He acts this
out, marching across the front of the stage.*) But . . . a couple
miles down the road he'll have stopped: 'Hold on, where
am I going for God's sake?' And he'll have thought for
a second and then – 'Ach, to hell with it, I'm *going*,
that's all that matters. I'll find out when I get there!'
(*Laughs. Drinks.*)

Aye, I bet that was it. Good luck to him, that's what I
say. (*Drinks again.*) One thing's for sure. You can only do
that when you're young. Once you get old, like me,
you're stuck. You're lucky if you get to take off just the
once in your life. (*Looks around, thinking back to the time he
took off, and landed in Blackden.*) I shouldn't complain.
Make sure you end up some place you want to end up,
that's my advice, cause once you're there (*Indicating
here.*), chances are you're stuck. You've got work, a wife
. . . responsibilities . . . habits . . . (*He drinks again.*) You
can't just drop all that.

(*He frowns, gives the flask a shake, raises it to his eye and tries to peer in: it's empty.*) Glory be, would you look at that. (*Puts his head back, upends the flask into it, taps it on the bottom to get the last few drops out.*) Nothing good lasts for ever. (*Stands on his kist, speaks a little solemnly, more like a minister than an auctioneer.*)

Ladies and gentlemen. The whisky is gone, and soon I will be too. Meanwhile, Dod o Goodman's is dead and buried. His goods and gear are displenished, sold for pennies and scattered to all corners of the civilised world. And Banchory. The croft itself is bought by a couple from Edinburgh, the Brindles, who're gutting it and getting it up as an artist's studio or something. (*Can I pick and choose who I sell to? No.*) (*Goes to take a drink, remembers it's empty.*) My whisky is gone. Did I say that? Well, my wife, Sandra, is gone, for thenight at least, to her sister's in Inverurie. That's what she *says*, anyroad. Christ, maybe she's going to disappear too! (*Mutters:*) Here's hoping.

(*Steps down, bends a little unsteadily to pick up his kist, then starts to leave. He pauses.*) Oh aye, and Patrick Hunter is gone ... who knows where. I doubt he's not run off with Sandra, anyway! (*Laughs.*) Eh, was I going to tell you something about him? (*Frowns.*) I think I was. But what? Well. (*Waves the flask around, walks off.*) See you later ...

Scene Five
Sometimes stories aren't enough

This time, **Shona** *appears with her chef's jacket unbuttoned, some kind of vest underneath. She is more relaxed now, smoking a skinny hand-rolled fag. She still tends to talk in those short jaggy sentences, but it doesn't seem quite so hostile any more: it's just the way her mind works.*

Shona   So, picture the scene. Blackden village hall, the Young Farmers' Club stovie dance. Beer stains on the

dance floor, plaster flaking off the walls where the
damp's getting in. And a hundred and twenty-odd
farmers, cheuchters, sheep-shaggers, girlfriends, wives,
bidie-ins, hoodlums, and drunks giving it laldie. Actually,
it's daft to give drunks a separate listing, cause by the
back of ten, when I got there with the stovies, *everybody*
was drunk just about. And so the dancing had begun!
Christ, this is Scotland after all: can't expect anyone to
dance *sober*. Not the men, anyroad.

So: keyboard, accordion and guitar on stage, and some
fat sweaty bastard belting out, 'She taught me how to
yodel, yodel-odel-ee, yodel-odel-ee . . .' The floor's skity
as an ice-rink with Slipperene, and aabody's doing the
Canadian Barn Dance, or some crap like that. All the
local bears are there: Brian Milne, coming on like the
Doric Casanova as usual; Dek Duguid, otherwise known
as Mr Misery From The Forestry; and John Wilson *not*
sloshing out the stovies himself surprise surprise, but
sooking up to this posh couple that spent a fortune off
the à la carte menu earlier on. Southern folk – from
Glasgow or Edinburgh, somewhere like that – bought
some old ruin they're going to do up as a
photographer's studio.

Anyway I've washed my hands of the stovies, and I'm
about to wash my hands of the whole fucking do, when
some daft bastard walks right into me, sends his stovies
flying! You guessed it: Patrick Hunter. Tan-ta-ra. Paddy
to his pals. Though as it happens his pals have all
waltzed off and left him with nothing but a pint and a
plate of greasy tatties for company.

He slagged off the stovies for being ower watery, but I
just laughed. 'Stovies should be thick enough,' he says,
'that you could dance a Strip the Willow with a plate in
each hand and never spill a drop. None of this calfie's
skitters!'

I just laughed again. 'Slag me as much as you like,
Paddy,' I said. 'I'm off duty as of ten minutes ago, so I
don't give a shit what you say.'

(*Explaining to the audience, amused at articulating the split so clearly.*) See, there's Shona Findlay the chef, and Shona Findlay the human being: two different folk. Aye, and they hate each other's guts. Which can be a bittie confusing, cause the human being keeps getting the chef into trouble by trying to make an appearance during working hours, and the chef keeps barging in during the human being's sociable hours, shagged out and bad fucking tempered!

Like earlier ... Cause I have to admit it, it does kind of wind me up working in that kitchen. The heat of it, the sweat. The way you've nothing to do for an hour and then twenty covers all order at fucking once ...

Anyway, Paddy's thanking me for the pie for his granny and granda. 'Compliments to the chef!' he goes.

'No,' I tell him. 'You mean, to the human being!' (*Pause; she wants the audience to get the distinction.*)

Anyway, it turns out that he's deeved of the do as well, and he's needing home. So I say I'll give him a lift. I mean, anyone would've done the same: I wasn't *meaning* anything by it. I bide out the same road as he does, a couple miles further on, so ... anyway, I don't need to fucking explain this do I? *I just said I'd give him a lift.* Full stop. And we were just fooling around in the car park, the two of us – he was slagging me off for being loud, right, so I grabs ahold of his lug to yell in it – when all of a sudden he turns round and before I know it my mouth – my lips, right, pouted up and ready to shout – they're touching his! (*She mimes it.*) Aye, lip-to-lip contact! I just laughed – I mean, it's a total fucking accident – there's nothing in it. But Paddy kind of starts getting a bit carried away, goes to put his arms round me, right there in the car park! And I'm like, *please*! (*Mimes pushing him away.*) I mean, not that he's not a fine enough loon, but ... me and Bobby, Bobby Bastard, we've been going out for *years*. Five years! Since we were bairns. Paddy kens that. He kens there could *never* be anything between me and him. Bobby would kill him! He'd kill me! (*She thinks about this for a second, fishes out a baccy tin, her hands slightly shaky. She makes another roly, and lights it. Maybe she's imagining at this point a life with somebody who's a fine enough loon, rather than a bastard.*)

Anyway, anyway. We get in the car and drive away out of the village, across the Clattering Briggie, up the brae. And we're just blethering about this and that, he's making me laugh about something, and ... I don't ken why, but I start telling him this story. Cause I can feel him looking at me as I'm driving. Not in a creepy way or anything, I mean it's quite fine in a way, but just *looking*; so I think to myself, I'll give him something to look at – or listen to, anyway. I'll tell him a story! (*Frowns, examining her motives.*) Aye. So I start telling him this story about me working late the week afore – Hallowe'en night! – and what I saw as I drove home ... (*She really gets into the tale, telling it very effectively.*)

'I was working till midnight on Hallowe'en,' I say, 'and by the time I headed home the village was dead: not a soul around. Somebody letting their dog pish on the manse gate and that's it. But ...' And I put on a kind of spooky voice here. 'But I'd just passed the kirk, right, when something caught my eye, made me slow and stop, made me look again into the woods behind the kirk. There was a light there.'

'There's no houses there,' says Paddy.

'I ken, but I'm telling you, there was a light in the middle of the trees, right in the depths of Kirk Woods. There was a light burning: a fire.' He's really looking at me now! 'Listen,' I go. 'Mind there's a kind of forestry track into the woods, half a mile or so on from the kirk?'

'The old drove road,' he goes.

'Aye, whatever. Well, there's a couple old cars and a van parked in there, pulled well in off the road, right under the trees. *Strange* ... And the gate at the end of the track was pulled shut after them. *Stranger* ... So what do I do Paddy? I stop the car. Why? Cause I'm a

daft bitch with nose problems, right? So, I got out of the
car, and I went ... to investigate ...' I really had him
hooked by this time, you should've seen his face! 'And
what did I find? The car engines were still warm, and
from deeper in the woods, there came glimmers of
firelight ... and strange noises.'
'What sort of noises, Shona?'
(*She's putting the story across very vividly in her voice and
movements, to the audience in the present more than to Patrick in
the past: it should be genuinely spooky.*) 'It was a kind of a
singing, but with a thumping in it as well: like a drum
or something. Hubba hubba wubba wubba hulla hulla
wulla wulla ... So, I walked on past the cars, going
deeper into the woods. I felt like I was being *drawn* into
the noise ... I kept on for five minutes or so, along the
track to start with, and then right amongst the trees, all
the time the firelight getting closer and the voices getting
louder. And it wasn't singing, more of a kind of
chanting, and maybe not a drum, maybe just feet
thumping on the ground as they ... *danced around the
bonfire.*'
'Wow!' he goes.
'I was *feart*,' I says, and I really meant it, I was feart just
telling it! 'Feart that they'd smell me out or something,
sense I was there and come after me and catch me and
... I don't know what. So I was just creeping up,
always on the point of turning and running, trying to be
as quiet as I could. Then I got about twenty metres
away: that was close enough, close enough ... to see.'
He's like ... (*Mimes mouth hanging open.*) 'To see what?'
'Half a dozen folk, women and a man, dancing round
the fire ... *completely naked* ... in front of this big kind of
altar stone ...'
Now he's like ... (*Even-more-astonished mime.*) He's
swallowing every word! Christ, I was so convincing, I
was just about believing the tale myself! (*Pause.*) By this
time, we're outside The Strath, Helen's old house, so I
stop the car. He just sits there. 'What happened next?'

he whispers. 'Was there . . . a body on the altar? A *sacrifice?*'

'No,' I said. 'Nothing like that. They were just dancing about, chanting, grabbing hold of each other and . . .'

'No sacrifice?'

No, there was definitely no sacrifice, I tell him. And he looks *disappointed*, almost.

'No body?' he says again.

I give him a nudge. 'I get it. You looking for a virgin, Paddy!'

(*Pause while he looks at her.*) 'You're joking,' he says. 'You're making the whole thing up.'

I tell him no. I tell him that when I got home at last, past midnight, and put the lights on, I could see the *evidence*: grass stains on my knees from where I'd been crawling through the woods, dirt and mould from the ground rubbed into my hands. (He's looking at me again.) 'And my whole body felt . . . (*She gives an ecstatic sigh and shudder.*) . . . *drained.*'

I tell you: I deserve a fucking Oscar! And Paddy's looking at me, mouth open, red in the face, and I wonder what he's going to say. And he says:

(*Hoarse.*) 'Do you want to come in for a cup of coffee?'

(*She laughs.*) Did I want to come in for a cup of coffee! (*More laughter at the boy's idiocy.*) No, I didn't, I said. I was too . . . *shagged out.*

And I did this big yawn, then leant across him, and opened his door.

'Goodnight Patrick,' I said.

'Will you not come in?' he goes. 'I need to . . . talk.'

'I bet you do,' I said. 'Going to tell me all your secrets, eh?' (*Thinking of secret loves, etc.*)

'I don't believe in secrets,' he says. 'You've told me yours . . .'

' "So I'll tell you mine"?' I laughed. 'Sweet dreams, Paddy.'

(*She considers the implications of his, thinks back over her recent scorn. She stands there for a moment, looking rueful, even regretful, now, then starts to walk off.*) I hope he does have sweet dreams. He deserves them. All he got from me was stories. Not even secrets! Just stories. (*She pauses at the edge of the stage, and says:*) Sometimes stories aren't enough. Sometimes you need someone to tell you ... real life. (*She steps off, pauses as* **Brian** *passes her on his way to the stage; she speaks again.*) I haven't seen him since then. Friday midnight. But other folk have, I ken, lots of folk: Saturday, Sunday morning. Ask them. I'm not holding back at all – it's just, I don't think I've really much ... I can say.

Scene Six
This bugger's got hell of a deep roots

Brian *is pretty much the same as before, except he's got on a baseball cap, and a pair of rigger gloves: work gear. He is still open and keen to communicate with the audience, though as this scene goes on it seems more and more that he didn't really understand what his friend was talking about half the time. Nor does he seem to get what* **Shona***'s talking about: he looks at her legs, frowns, waits for her to sit down.*

Brian   First thing Saturday morning, I was out in the muckle park below Goodman's Croft. My father bought the land after he died, see. From the lawyers. I don't ken who gets the money. Not old Dod, that's for sure. No pooches in a shroud! Anyway, I was clearing stones off the top of it. Hell of a rummlie. Don't reckon Dod had been over it for twenty year! Anyway, next thing I ken, here's Paddy coming pleitering across the park towards me. 'What're you doing?' he says. 'Picking tatties?' He was joking. I hope.
I got him to help me with this one big bugger of a stone. I couldn't move it an inch even, so I got him to come and grab ahold of one end, and me the other, and we tried to get it rocking, ken, to work it free of its socket. (*Squats down, pulls the gloves on tight, mimes the action.*)

Him pushing down, me pulling up, him pulling up, me pushing down ... (*His face red with the effort.*) JESUS! (*He releases the stone, jumps clear.*)

'JCB job,' I goes.

'You'll never move the bugger,' he says. 'This one's roots go *all* the way down.'

(*He shrugs at Paddy's daft imagination.*) He does speak some right shite sometimes. I mind one time, this time a year ago more or less, and we came out of the Old Mill late one night; the frost had come down, the ground was all icy. We started sliding up and down the square, ken, round and round Queen Victoria's horse trough, and then suddenly Paddy stops stock still, this look on his face. (*Mimes a look of horror.*) 'What's up?' I said.

'Mind when we were kids and we played at slidies?' he said.

'Aye.'

'Aye, well. Mind how folk were always saying, "Stop that boys, or you'll fall and split your head open!"?'

'Aye.'

'Well, I used to hate it when the dominie or my dad or anyone said that, cause I could just imagine it, ken. I could just imagine speeding along that slide, then SKITE, my feet go out from under me and CRACK my head hits the playground concrete. Then it would split open, my head, come right into two pieces, like a chocolate Easter egg with all the Smarties spilling out the middle. I could just see the two halves of my head splitting apart and falling to each side! Jesus! And there'd be me, my brains starting to spill out, and I'd have to hold the two halves of my head, one in each hand, and cram the brains in with my thumbs, and I'd have to go running along to the teachers' staffroom to get a bit of sellotape to wrap around my head to hold it all together.'

Well what would you do if somebody said that to you? I just laughed!

And Paddy looked at me kind of hopeful, 'Did you have

the same idea too?' he said. 'If you ever opened
your head, a whole *load* of stuff would come pouring
out?'

'You're joking!' I went. 'I was just laughing cause I was
reminded how you were always a weird bastard, even
when you were fucking seven!'

And then we both started mucking about again, sliding
back and forwards across the street all the way home.
Well, I slid; he just walked. (*Shakes his head, picturing this
happy scene.*) You see what I mean though? He's my
oldest pal, but I've still got no idea what he's talking
about half the time!

(*Frowns, thinking. Gets down on his hunkers.*) But I've just
thought of something, right. What about this? Eh . . . (*He
stands up again.*) Hold on . . . Right. He was always good
at school and that, ken. I mean he wasn't a swot or
anything, but he just kind of sat there like a big sponge
and soaked it all in, everything the teachers told him,
everything the dominie told him, and his mother and
father, and his granny and grandad. That's what Paddy
was like . . . (*Does an impression of him: open mouth, eyes like
saucers: listening, as intently as he did to* **Shona**.)
Spongeman . . .

Here's what I was thinking. Say that's what you're like,
that's your character: you listen, and you believe what
you're tellt. All your life. What happens . . . when the
day comes . . . when you see through all the shite. If
you suddenly don't *believe* any more? What do you do?
I'll tell you: you go down to the river, fill your pooches
with rocks, and jump in the Dooker Pool.

How about that for a theory?

Fuck it. It's probably shite. He's not in the Dooker,
anyway, cause I looked. That would've been a turn-up,
eh? But nuh: nothing exciting like that ever happens
here. (*Momentarily disappointed, he paces about; then he changes
the subject.*)

Let me tell you about the roup, though. Cause after a
while more on Goodman's old park, I'd cleared all of

the stones I could be arsed to, and headed up to the
croft to have a look at what was for sale. I wouldn't
have missed it for all the tea in Typhoo. It's a historic
occasion, you ken, when this happens: an old croft's
displenish sale. It's the passing of an old way of life, it's
the future turning up and booting the old ways out.
History! (*Pause.*) That's what Paddy used to say, anyway.
I think he reckoned it was a bad thing. So why he was
an apprentice auctioneer doing the bloody *selling* I don't
ken!

Anyway, roups are always good entertainment, that's for
sure: you can't beat them for hearing the latest news, for
seeing the hillbillies down from the mountains, for
watching two folk bid it out to the *death* just about over
a bucket of rusty nails or something – going up a penny
at a time: twenty pence I'd bid twenty, I'm bid twenty-
one, twenty-one, twenty-two, twenty-three pence on my
right here – and the two guys'll be getting all worked
up, looking daggers at each other over the heads of this
bucket of rust and their pocket-money bids. (*Laughs.*)
Better than a night at the pictures, a roup! And it's free!
(*Pause.*) Unless you get carried away and buy some shite
yourself, like.

Anyway, old Bill Murray, Bill the Booze, was up on his
box, jogging about, getting into the swing of things. A
beer-belly dancer, Paddy called him once. (*Mimes* **Bill***'s
big belly swinging about.*) Anyway, Bill's up there on his
kist in the middle of the court, calling out the lot numbers,
whipping the bidding along. (*Imitation:*) 'Bidalalalala-
wibalalala-fiveafivea-wiba-kakaka . . .' (*It turns into the*
William Tell *tune for a few seconds.*) And there's folk
gathered in all about him, except for a small clearing
right in front of him. And that's Paddy's stamping
ground.

(*Making us see all this with his actions.*) All the lots were
laid out in dreels in the old tractor shed, and Paddy
would wait till Bill shouted out a number, then he'd go
flying into the shed and come back into the body of the

kirk with the lot in his arms – a hosepipe and stirrup
pump, a roll of barbed wire, a rusty neep-hasher, half a
hundredweight of rat poison – and he'd bear it about
the circle, hefting it up so that even the folk at the back
could see what they were wasting their money on. And
as soon as Bill whacked his foot down on the kist, and
the thing was sold, Paddy would have to get the buyer's
name, and write it on the lot, and chuck the lot back in
the shed and come running out with the next one.
(*Laughs.*) Hard work! Don't you just love watching
somebody else do it! Aye, half an hour of that and the
sweat was pishing off him.

And then, just as Paddy comes out of the shed and
starts wandering about with lot 153, these two wee
flagons, there's a roaring noise: a big gold yuppie jeep
comes shooting up the track to the croft, skids round
into the court and slams on its brakes just half a yard
from mowing down the outside rings of the steer. God's
sake! Folk are muttering and moaning, and Bill Murray's
frozen in mid-bid. (*He mimes the pose.*) Everybody's
wondering, who the hell's this idiot? When out steps . . .
the mannie Brindle! Flat cap, wax jacket and . . . green
wellies. Oh aye: the full fucking rig-out. The boy gives
Bill a wave. (*Posh voice.*) 'Sorry I'm late Mr Murray:
unavoidable I'm afraid. Do you know the nearest fax is
seven *miles* away? Ridiculous! All going well I trust?'
This was right in the middle of the roup! All the folk
standing gowping at him like . . . cows over a dyke. But
he doesn't seem to care! Murray just goes, 'Oh yes sir
Mr Brindle sir three bags full sir, everything's absolutely
spiffing.'

Bill (*shouting from the audience*) Rubbish!

Brian (*loudly*) Anyway . . . 'Top hole,' says Brindle, or
something, and he kind of looks around and beams at
aabody. Then he spots Paddy standing there, these two
wee milk flagons on his shoulders that the woman from

the goat farm over at Kinker's just bid three-fifty for.
And Brindle goes, 'Ah! Aquarius! The water carrier!' A
few folk laugh, and Brindle grins – he doesn't realise
folk aren't laughing at his joke, they're laughing at *him*
for being such an arsehole – and Paddy goes, 'No,
they're not for water, they're for milk: for taking milk
out of one thing and putting it into another.'
'Like out of a cow and into your coffee?' says Brindle.
'Excellent: I'll bid twenty pounds. Twenty pounds the
pair, Mr Murray.'
And Bill's looking black affronted . . .

Bill I *was* black affronted.

Brian That's what I said. But all you said was, 'Eh,
any more bids?'
'Not at that price,' says the woman from the goat farm.
'Sold,' said Bill. (**Brian** *slaps his foot down in imitation of*
Bill'*s half-hearted stomp.*)

Bill For God's sake! (*Gets out of his seat and heads for the
stage.*)

Brian 'Excellent,' says Brindle. 'Always happy to join
in the spirit of things. Boy: bring them round to the
kitchen later.'
Aye! You should've seen Paddy's face at that!
(*Confidentially.*) We've had a lot of arguments about folk
like that in the past, me and Paddy: (*Venomously.*) white
settlers. He makes on he doesn't mind them! (*Shakes his
head in disbelief.*) Coming up here, flashing around their
cash and their fancy cars . . . and their fancy women.
Well, I reckon this lot are the final straw: either they've
finally driven Paddy out, or else they've brought him to
his senses. Could be he's up at Goodman's now:
battering the mannie Brindle to death with Bill's kist!
(*Laughs.*) Chance would be a fine thing. Then Marjorie
would *have* to dance with me at the next Young
Farmers' do. (*Quite a nasty raunchy roar.*) Yes!

Scene Seven
His boss, after all, not his bloody father

Bill *has sobered up since the last time we saw him; maybe he is even feeling a bit hungover. He's still a natural performer, and talks very confidently, but he's not quite as beaming and hearty as he was earlier. He sets down the kist right next to* **Brian***, gives it a pat.*

Bill   What were you saying about incomers?

Brian *sneers and walks off.*

Bill *(steps up and addresses the audience, with a scornful glance at* **Brian***'s back)*   Let's get back down to earth here.

Brian *(speaking from the audience, just before he sits down; perplexed verging on angry)*   What's he like, eh? Paddy: what's he like? Here's me, his oldest pal, his oldest and *best* pal . . . and I'm talking to him *all* weekend, and he never *once* mentions he's going to take off. But that's what he does. He doesn't stand and fight the rot. He disappears. Comes to the dance, the pub, the curling, does bugger all the same as the rest of us all weekend, then suddenly . . . Sunday afternoon: 'Where's Paddy?' 'Anybody seen Paddy?' Nuh! And nobody's seen him since. He's off, away, out of Blackden. *(As if it's the biggest betrayal imaginable.)* Out of Blackden.

Bill   Get a grip, pal. Let's get back to reality, eh? *(Thinks, remembers where to start.)* I gave Patrick a lift home after we'd finished clearing up at Goodman's. *(Holds up a finger to stop himself.)* There's two parts to this. The first part is: he arrived on his old bike as usual in the morning, but . . . he couldn't leave on it. Ahem. Because, owing to a . . . eh, clerical error, eh . . . och, to hell with it. *(Opens his palms to the audience in admission of guilt.)* I sold his bike off by mistake at the roup. Well, I mean to say: it was a rusty old wreck of a thing, fitted in just fine with the rest of the shite lying about

there. He should've known better than to leave it lying
against the dyke like that. I mean, obviously nobody's
going to *steal* it, I'm not saying lock it up, but . . . you
can understand how it happened . . . (*He acts it out.*)
Patrick's inside the house helping Sandra with the tea-
urn or something, and I'm leading the folk along to the
park where all the implements are lined up. And on the
way along the track, we pass this old message bike
propped up against Dod's dyke, just sitting there. Now, I
couldn't miss a chance like that, the chance of a few
bob! – so I just jumped up on the dyke, planted my
boot on the saddle of the bike, and auctioned the
bugger off. Five pound five pound, I'm bid five at the
back five at the back and six pound six bid seven bid
seven bid I'm bid eight bid . . . You get the idea. I
whipped it up to twenty-one quid. (*A wink.*) A good
price.
I said that to Patrick when he found it was gone, last
thing. 'It's a good price lad,' I said. 'For an antique like
that. Not exactly the latest model is it?'
'Twenty-one quid?' he said.
'Well, less commission.'
He blew his top at that. Quite right really, I suppose.
He wanted me to get it back for him, but how could I?
I'd sold it to the butcher over in Tarland: I couldn't
drive twenty miles and ask the boy for the thing back,
not after he'd paid good money for it. So. Patrick was
not happy, he . . . (*Frowns.*) Here, I never thought of that
before: maybe that's where he is: walking over to
Tarland to get his bloody bike back! That'll be it! Jesus
Christ! (*Laughs, then looks serious again.*) Of course, if he left
Blackden first thing yesterday morning, he should've
easily got there by the afternoon, even if he wasn't
hitching. And I ken I said the bike was a wreck, but it
wasn't *that* bad: he would definitely have made it home
by now. So, that can't be where he is. Unless he rubbed
the butcher up the wrong way and got chopped up into
sausagemeat or something. No. (*Suddenly annoyed.*) Christ,

I've got a big livestock sale on Wednesday: two hundred sheep and a hundred or so store cattle. How can I handle that by myself? I need Patrick to be there. Where the hell *is* he?

(*Pause while he calms down.*) I just don't ken. I'm his boss, after all, not his bloody father. (*He frowns with embarrassment at what he's just said, covers it up by taking out his hip-flask for the first time and drinking a long drink.*) Ah! (*He stomps his foot down, cheery again.*) Sold! To the man with the single malt!

There was something else I was going to tell you. (*Thinks.*) Oh aye. I said I gave him a lift home, but actually I only took him halfway there, and then he made me stop and let him out. I thought he was joking to start with: it was half four or something, pretty much dark, and freezing cold with the clearness of the sky. I was just saying to him something about the curling season coming in with all these hard frosts, and the next thing I ken he's shouting, 'STOP, STOP!' I kind of slowed down: worried I'd run something over, but no: 'Will you stop the van?' he goes. 'This is far enough, I'm needing out.'

'It's a mile to the village and another mile to your house,' I said. 'I'll easy take you.'

But he's already unfastening his seatbelt and getting the door open. So I stop, and he steps out – WHOOMPH! – straight into the bloody ditch! (*Laughs.*) Luckily there was nothing in it but leaves. 'Are you all right lad?' I says. (*Leaning over to see out the passenger door.*) But he doesn't answer: he's already heading off into the bloody Kirk Woods! There's this track through the trees there, an old cattle drove road if I mind right, and Patrick's striding off down it quite the thing. 'Where are you going?' I shout after him, but he doesn't answer, just keeps walking.

(*He looks around the audience, as if looking for an explanation. Then he shrugs, takes a sip of his whisky, and goes for a walk around the stage himself. From up the back, he starts talking*

again, gradually coming to the front once more.)
But that wasn't the last I saw of him. Cause I was right
about the weather: it *had* got cold enough for the curling
to start. We – the Blackden Curling Club – we flooded
the tennis courts a couple weeks ago, but it had never
quite frozen up. Till Saturday night. So, the call went
out, and about ten o'clock we all met up there. Oh, it's
a great feeling, the first curling of the season. Like an
Old Firm game and Hogmanay rolled into one.
(*This is obviously a great joy to him: he really gets into it, rubbing
his hands in the imagined cold, etc.*) It's always at night, of
course, and you're out past the pleasure park there, no
streetlamps, so it's completely dark as you walk out. And
you hear the stones clinking together in your bag, and
your breath crackling in the air . . . and the only light
comes from the stars up in the sky. Till suddenly . . .
you go over the wee hill between the park and the
curling and POW: a blaze of whiteness! You look down,
and the rink's so brightly lit – floodlights up in the trees
shining down on the ice – that it looks like it's a little
bright world all on its own, floating away through black
space . . . *Heaven!*
Then your eyes get used to it, and you see, nah: it's just
two tennis courts, flooded and frozen, and there's teams
of folk skiting stones up and down, and other folk
sweeping like crazy to speed the stones up, and other
folk, the skips, telling them when to sweep and when to
rest. And the spectators are shouting instructions too, or
giving the odd cheer when somebody hits one right to
the tee, or cracks an egg. And there's bottles being
passed about, and flasks of tea – and the whole village is
there more or less, especially on the first night of the
season, and everybody's just having a *magic* time.
Except Patrick Hunter. I don't understand it: his father
was always a great man for the curling, a skip since he
was sixteen so I'm told. But Patrick's just not interested!
(*Shakes his head in disbelief.*) I don't know why. I mean I
don't suppose I've ever asked him, it's not like it's a big

secret or anything. Hih! He always used to say he didn't
have any secrets. Usually I'd be asking him what he got
up to at the weekend, where he'd been, how blootered
he'd got, who he'd got off with . . . 'Is that *all* you did?'
I'd say after a while. And he'd go, 'No, there's more.'
'Secrets!' I'd say. 'Holding back the juicy bits!' 'There's
no secrets, Bill,' Patrick'd say, 'just questions you haven't
asked me yet.'

Anyway. One of the questions I never asked him was,
how come your dad was such a big curler, and you
don't ever play? Ah! The roaring game, we call it! The
stones across the ice . . . Blackden's answer to the
Hampden roar!

(*He's transported back to the scene.*) I walked down into
heaven. Everybody else, playing or just watching, is
having a ball, but Patrick's just standing at the edge,
leaning against one of the monkey puzzles with the
floodlights in it, and staring at the ground. Well, it turns
out I have to wait ten minutes or so before I can get
onto a rink, so I wander over for a blether with him:
'Patrick,' I goes, 'fine night. Have a drink!' But he
wouldn't. So I did. (*And he does again.*) 'Come on Paddy,'
I said. 'Cheer up: it might never happen! Eh? Ha ha!'
But he doesn't look any cheerier.

'This is it, Bill,' he says – and I let him call me that,
even though I'm the boss and he's just the apprentice,
none of this Mr Murray rubbish – 'This is it: it already
has happened.'

'What are you talking about, lad?' I say.

'Well,' he goes. 'Ken when I headed off into the Kirk
Woods this afternoon? Ken what I found? A stone
circle.'

'I hate to disappoint you, Patrick,' I said. 'But there's
nothing new about that: it's been there since I first
moved here, twenty year at least.'

'It's been there a lot longer than that,' he says. 'I ken
that fine. But here's something that hasn't been there so
long: a bonfire. In the middle of the stone circle, there's

the remains of a big bonfire: ashes, half-burnt branches, a hearth of stones. And all the grass round about is flattened – just like somebody's been walking or . . . *dancing* about there.'

I told him it was probably just the hippies camping there again. Or some kids sneaking out there to drink Hooch where their folks can't see them. But Patrick wasn't having any of it. No, he goes. It wasn't that, it was . . . well . . . most of the time you think you ken what's true, and what's a lie; what's a story and what's real. But sometimes something crops up that's both at the same time. Truth and a lie. If the words weren't there to label the different bits, you wouldn't be able to tell them apart. (*Pause while* **Bill** *looks at him in astonishment and incomprehension, then:*)

'Patrick,' I said. 'What the hell are you talking about?'

He looks at me. Laughs. And suddenly he changes: leans off the tree, claps me on the shoulder, a big grin across his chops:

'Bill,' he says. 'You've always been straight with me, so I'll be straight with you. This afternoon, while you were along at the implement park, the mannie Brindle offered me a job.'

'Bastard!' I said. 'Poaching my workers!'

'He's setting up a kind of Scottish gift business in the old croft,' said Patrick. 'Beach towels with pictures of Great Scottish Battlefields of the Olden Days printed on them. And postcards: Ravenscraig Steelworks, Linwood Car Plant, Piper Alpha – it's a series called "The Sun Sets On The Great Scottish Industries". A kind of nostalgia thing, ken? And he wants me to go and work for him: packing them up, selling them to folk in all the tourist shops in the north-east.'

I was gobsmacked, so I took a drink to clear my head. (*Another drink.*) I never liked that man, I never trusted him, the way he thinks he's so . . . better. That's not the way we do things about here! 'Who'll I get instead of you?' I said. 'I *need* an apprentice: there's no way I can . . .'

'BILL!' he shouts. 'Don't worry! I tellt him to stick his
job. I wouldn't work for an arsehole like him in a
million years.'

And I'm like, 'Wha . . . you . . . why . . . hey . . .
YEAHHH!' (*He punches the air with relief.*) And – I don't
ken what got into me: too much Grouse maybe – but I
grabbed hold of him (*He mimes it.*) and started waltzing
around, I was that happy! Yippee! Right to the tee,
Patrick!

(And before you ask, I did check up at Goodman's
today to see if he'd gone there after all. No: and Mr
Brindle got a bit worked up at the mention of his name,
even. Apparently he really did tell him to stick his job
up his arse!)

Anyway, back at the curling . . . I got shouted over to
the end rink: my game was about to start. 'I've got to
go, lad,' I said to him. 'But thanks. Thanks.' I started
unzipping my bag to get out the stones. 'Here,' I said,
'maybe have a game with you later on, eh? Will I put
your name down?'

'No way Bill,' he said. 'You'll not catch me out on that
ice: I'd only fall and split my head open. And who
knows what'd start pishing out of it . . .'

Scene Eight
The great thing and the scary thing

Heather *comes on, more poised than she was at the end of her
last appearance. She speaks from the edge of the stage.*

Heather I do.

Bill *walks off as she comes on. She's obviously been worrying
about Patrick since we last saw her: her brow is furrowed, her
cigarette already lit. No chair this time.*

Heather Do you know what today is?

Bill   Monday. And the cattle mart's on Wednesday.

Heather   Aye, but what else? (**Bill** *shrugs, and she answers.*) It's a year ago today that Alec Hunter died. (**Bill** *stops, looks at her.*) That's why Moira's gone away for this long weekend: so she won't have to be in the house on the anniversary . . . of the death.

Bill   Jesus. I didn't know. I mean I knew it was around now sometime, but . . .

Heather (*shakes her head*)   I forgot as well.

Bill   Aye, cause I was at the funeral, I should've remembered. It was the middle of that bitter cold spell: ice everywhere, the earth like glass. They had to postpone the burial, remember, cause the ground was too hard for Bobby Bastard to dig. Hard as rock, the soil in the cemy.

Shona   Aye, even when he got through the turf the soil was frozen underneath. (*Confidentially, this is a secret.*) Bobby couldn't get down six feet. That grave's nowhere near as deep as it's supposed to be.

Heather   It was a terrible time. And I'd forgotten. Caught up in my own problems I suppose. It wasn't till Patrick reminded me . . . and that was too late. (**Bill** *and* **Shona** *sit down as* **Heather** *looks at them: she's being allowed to have her final say.*) Hih, it *was* late: half four on Sunday morning. (*Looks at her watch.*) Thirty- . . . nine hours ago. It maybe doesn't sound much. But in a place like Blackden, thirty-nine *minutes* is a long time not to find somebody you're looking for.
(*Thinks back to the last time she saw him.*) I was angry to start with, but then I saw the state of him. Looked like he'd slept in a ditch all night. Blue with cold. I felt sorry for him then. So I took him in, gave him a cup of coffee, got the Raeburn roaring. Of course, I wanted to ken what the hell was going on: you don't turn up at somebody's door at half four in the morning – miles

from your own home, in muddy breeks and hair like a
haystack – unless something's going on.
So he told me: he had something important to tell me,
he said. What's that? I asked. He looked at me. Politics,
he said. *Eh?* He said it was about that political
discussion we'd been having, about me trying to get him
to come along to SNP branch meetings. Well, there's a
time and a place, I know, and this wasn't either. But . . .
it wasn't like I'd anybody else to talk to. (*Shrugs, takes a
drag.*) So I settled down for a long talk. (*Something occurs to
her. She walks off, picks up her chair, and comes back on with it.
She sits down.*)
And he says, 'Aye, I've been thinking about it, and I've
decided, so I thought I better let you know: I'm *not*
coming along to your meetings, I'm *not* interested in
your kind of politics, I'm not interested in the Scottish
National Party. That's it.'
'What?' I said. 'Pardon? "That's it"?'
'Aye,' he said. 'So, I'll just finish my coffee, and be off.'
Can you believe it? I wouldn't let him go. I tellt him he
wasn't getting away with waking me up in the middle of
the night – Christ, I'd only gone to bed at one! – and
telling me two sentences about why he *wasn't* going to
take up my suggestion.
'You are involved whether you like it or not, Patrick,' I
said to him. 'You were born here, your folks were born
here; you live and work here. All your friends are here.
You've got the accent. You've got the mind-set. You're
a Blackdenner. You *are* involved.'
(*Pause.*) 'That's not involved,' he says. 'That's entangled.
That's trapped.'
That stopped me in my tracks: made me think. And
while I was thinking, he was getting angry.
He's just Patrick Hunter, he says. It doesn't matter
where he comes from, or where his folks come from.
He's just him. It doesn't matter where he works, or
where he lives, he's still him, *wherever*. (*Becoming animated
as she impersonates him.*) 'My accent's just an accident. *It's*

not me. I don't have a mind-set; my mind *isn't* set.
Concrete sets, my mind isn't like that: it's like . . . like
water: it can freeze into ice, or boil into steam, or just
be water and flow along anywhere.'
'Patrick,' I said. 'Listen . . .'
'I live in Blackden,' he said. 'It doesn't live in me.'
'Does it not?'
'No.'
'Does it not?'
And this is where I disagreed with him, see. Cause I've
lived here longer than him: all my life. Well, he's lived
here all his life as well, I suppose, but my life's twice as
long as his, so . . . I've seen things he hasn't, maybe.
Like, with old folk especially. Eighty-year-old women
who've never *once* got to do what they want or say what
they want. It's a hell of a backward place, in some ways.
Eighty-year-old women who've done nothing but look
after their bastard men for sixty years. Or even if their
men *aren't* bastards, even if they're decent . . . Folk here
– aye, and not just the old folk – folk always keep their
emotions under lock and key. Chained up. Never a bit
of freedom to say what you really think or really feel.
Too busy just *getting by* for that. I don't want to be like
that. I'm *not* like that. But it is hard to break out of it. I
said to Patrick: it's a struggle to break those chains, if
you're born with them round your heart.
But Patrick didn't get it; he shook his head. (*Pause.*) 'I
can do anything I like,' he said. (Could a woman say
that? I don't know. Anyway:) 'I can do anything I like,'
he said. 'I can *be* anything I like. That's the great thing.
That's the scary thing. You *can* do anything you like, as
long as you're willing to live with it afterwards.'
And he gave me this look. And for a second I thought
there were tears starting to come up in his eyes. But no.
He just looked at me. I leant towards him, fixed him.
'Right, Patrick,' I said. 'Where've you been thenight?
What's been going on? What the *hell* are you doing in
my kitchen at half four on a Sunday morning?'

And here's what he said. (*She shows Paddy in a kind of reverie. He's obviously been thinking a lot, and the following memory is important to him.*) He said, 'Me and Dek and Bri used to be always building gang huts and dens when we were kids. It was our favourite thing to do in the summer, I think: build a den all day till you were hot and covered in muck, then bike down the denside and jump in the Dooker to cool off.'

Brian (*standing up in the audience*) That's true. We built platforms up trees, we dug holes in the ground and roofed them with corrugated iron. We made wigwams of branches, with bracken woven in and out for the sides. We arranged circles of boulders for walls and told ourselves we'd built a castle. (*Getting enthusiastic, remembering the technical aspects of the building, maybe, and the good old comprehensible Paddy.*) One time, after a storm had knocked down a tree near The Strath, we built a den up against the roots of it – like massive fingers sticking up in the air. That was a good den, half the work had already been done for us. We finished it in no time, played in it all weekend.

Heather What happened to it?

Brian Paddy's dad came and sawed it up for firewood. They were all wrecked by parents or other kids or gamies or the weather. But we kept on building them. I don't ken why. We built them and then, after a day or a week, they got wrecked and we built another one. It didn't bother me. I mind Paddy got a bit upset about that tree one, but ... (*Shrugs.*) ... that's just the way things are. You can't just have kids going around building things and leaving them there – changing the face of the village. No, they've got to be knocked down. (*Pause.*) So if I'm ever out and I see some kids've built a den, I always smash it up. Doesn't take long. (*Sits, then immediately stands again.*) I'd do the same with some of these incomer bastards' bungalows if I could. Coming in here, *changing* the place. (*Shakes his head.*) Terrible. (*Sits* *down again.*)

Heather   'What are you getting at Patrick?' I said.
'Tonight I followed . . . this girl home after the curling.'
I must've been frowning, cause he shook his head,
laughed. 'Nothing bad,' he said. 'Just . . . we had a bit
of a thing, me and Shona. And then I hadn't seen her
all weekend. And I wanted to, I needed to. Because,
let's face it Heather, I'd already decided that I didn't
want Brindle's *new* job, that I was fed up with my *old*
job, that Bri doesn't ken what I'm talking about half the
time. I don't like *curling*, I can't *dance*, I can't get excited
about your politics. Let's face it, Heather: if there's no
future in me and . . . this girl, Shona, then there's *nothing*
for me in Blackden.'
I reached out, put my hand on top of his.
'And that's how it turned out. I went after her to try
and find out. I wasted my time. (*Pause.*) There's nothing
here any more.'
What about your family, I asked him.
'Helen's at the uni,' he said. 'Mother's away half the
time. My dad's . . . been dead for three hundred and
sixty-four days exactly. What I have, what I've had for a
year now, what me and nobody else has, is the memory,
the feeling, the memory of my dad lying there, dying.
'And the feeling, the feeling when he asked me to help
him die quicker. He couldn't ask my mother, couldn't
put that burden on her.
'But me . . . bastard! He put it on me!
'That's what Blackden is for me: it's the dead man's
burden.'

There is a second's silence, then **Shona** *gets up from her seat in
the audience, and speaks.*

Shona   I was putting a bag of rubbish out on Sunday
morning, and I spotted this hole in the ground. Bobby's
caravan's in a clearing in the woods, see, and over at
the edge of the clearing somebody had scrabbled a
hollow out of the earth. It was up against the roots of a

fallen tree. And they'd leant a couple pine branches between the earth and the roots. Just some kids building a den, I thought to myself. And then I shivered. Cause ken what it looked like? A grave.

Shona *sits down, and* **Heather**, *still on stage, talks again.*

Heather   So of course the first thing I blurts out is, 'So did you do it, Patrick? Did you do what your dad asked?' And he looks at me. 'Yes,' he says. (*Answering another question, or at least indicating in his* voice *that it's another question he's answering – though maybe he's answering* **Heather**'s *question too.*) 'Yes, there's going to have to be some changes. I'm too old for dens now,' he goes. 'And I'm far too young to be climbing into a grave, that's one thing for sure.'
(*Reaching out to take his hand.*) 'Nobody's going to put you in a grave,' I says.
'I thought . . .' he goes, 'it felt like . . . sometimes it felt like . . . the weight of my father was going to put me there. Dragging me down.'

Now **Brian** *stands up and speaks cheerily, unconcerned or unaware that he is breaking the mood.*

Brian   I mind another thing Paddy said. It was a Sunday afternoon a couple weeks ago, and we were that bored we were watching an Elvis film on BBC2. Elvis was this motorbiker in a fairground, and the trick he did was, he rode the Wall of Death. Round and round and round the big wooden barrel, faster and faster and faster . . . And Paddy says, 'Hey man, look at Elvis: he might as well be living in Blackden.'
'What are you talking about?' I said.
'Well, cooried down here with the hills all around, if you didn't watch out you'll spend your whole life whizzing round and round the walls of the den like Elvis on that contraption. Going a hell of a speed, but never actually getting anywhere. Round and round to the same places, round and round with the same people,

round and round with the same thoughts going round
and round in your head.'
'You're mad,' I said to him. Ken what he said?
He said, 'I'm not mad, just dizzy: eighteen years on the
Blackden Wall of Death!'

Brian *looks around for laughter, thinking this is stupid and
funny; then he sits down, and* **Heather** *talks again.*

Heather   I said to him, 'Well, I'm carrying the weight
as well now, Patrick. It won't be so heavy on you now.'
'I feel lighter,' he said. 'I feel like I can move.'
And he jumped up, got his coat on, headed for the
door.
'I can give you a lift home if you like,' I said. But he
said no – I told you this already – he'd had enough lifts
from folk to last him a lifetime. He was going to travel
under his own steam from now on.

Now **Bill** *stands up and talks.*

Bill   I'll tell you the worst of it. This is how soft I am,
right. On Sunday afternoon I went over to Tarland, and
knocked on the door of that butcher. 'There's been a
mistake,' I said to him. 'I shouldn't've sellt you that old
bike.'
'But you did,' he said, then he gave me this sly smile.
'And I've got very *attached* to it since yesterday.'
The tight-fisted bugger! I had to pay him thirty quid to
get it back! And then Patrick blinking well disappears,
leaves me with the rusty old wreck on my hands! What
am I going to do with it? Cover my losses, that's what!
Who'll start the bidding at twenty pounds? (*Pause.*) No?
Ten then? (*He waits in vain.*) A fiver, surely? Patrick
Hunter's bike! First bid of a pound secures! Hammer's
up . . .

*He looks around, his breath held. When nobody bids, he exhales,
lets his hands drop, sits down. On stage,* **Heather** *gets to her
feet.*

Heather   So I go with him to the door. It's still only about five, still pitch dark and freezing. But he's itching to get on, to get away, to get *moving*.

'Cheerio Heather,' he says to me, and he gives me a hug. And that's amazing too! A Scotsman showing affection!

I shiver. 'It's starvation out there,' I say to him. 'Hold on till I get you a scarf, some gloves or something.' He gives me a smile, so I duck into the hallway, rummage in the cupboard for a second. (*Pause.*) And when I turn back to the door, there he is, gone. (*Pause.*) He'd spoken. He'd passed the secret on to me. He'd broken those chains. (*Touches her heart.*) Just by telling me the story. The same story I'm telling you now.

I'd Rather Go Blind

Characters

Colin, *mid twenties*
Sally, *mid twenties*
Alec, *Sally's father, forties*
Rene, *Colin's mother, forties*

I'd Rather Go Blind was first performed by the Traverse Theatre, Edinburgh, on 15 October 1999, directed by Philip Howard, and subsequently toured in their Highland Shorts season

Darkness. Music plays loud: 'Hideaway' by Freddy King. After the first chorus, and as the lights fade up, **Colin** *and* **Sally** *come on stage from separate sides, sit on chairs. For the duration of the second chorus they just sit there, facing out. After about forty seconds, as the third chorus (walking bass line) starts to fade out,* **Sally** *speaks.*

Sally CRAP!

Colin I'd say our relationship's pretty good actually. Very good.

Sally You would.

Colin I've never had any complaints.

Sally Not that you've heard.

Colin No complaints at all.

Sally Amazing what you don't hear if you don't bloody listen.

Colin Course occasionally she gets on my nerves, like, but I don't make a big thing about it.

Sally Not big to you.

Colin I turn a blind eye.

Sally You shut me in the bedroom.

Colin That's what marriage is all about – you turn a blind eye to your wife's misdemeanours.

Sally Out of sight, out of mind – he shuts me in the bloody bedroom for hours on end.

Colin *laughs loudly at what she's just said.*

Sally He turns a blind eye to my black eye.

Colin I don't know what she's saying, I never fucking hit her.

Sally *scowls at him: the first direct look between them.*

Colin   Sorry! My language! I never *f-ing* hit her. (*Looks at her.*) Happy?

Sally   You're not supposed to do that.

Colin   I said sorry!

Sally   Not the fucking! The lying!

Colin   Who's fucking lying?

Sally   You are!

Colin   Oh fuck!

Sally   You're fucking lying!

Colin   Don't start!

Sally   Start what? It's you that's starting fucking lying! Start what?

Colin   Don't start the fucking accusations, that's what.

Sally   It's not accusations, it's truth.

Colin   Same fucking thing out of your mouth.

Sally   Oh aye, and whose mouth would you prefer?

Pause.

Colin   Bitch.

Sally   Bastard.

Colin   Ball-breaker.

Sally (*shouting*)   I'll get my father on to you!

Alec *comes storming on from* **Sally**'s *side of the stage, his face contorted with rage, strides straight over towards* **Colin**. **Colin** *jumps to his feet, lifts up his chair, holds it up as a barrier between him and* **Alec**. **Alec** *seizes the chair legs, and the two of them wrestle for a moment, each trying to overpower the other. As they do so, there's shouting along the lines of:*

Alec   Bastard, lying bastard, cheating bastard.

Colin   Alec, sit down, come on, sit down.

Sally *jumps up, runs over, grabs the chair.*

Sally   Come on youse two, no fighting.

Alec *and* **Colin** *both push her away.* **Sally** *goes back, grabs her dad by the shoulders, pulls him away.* **Colin** *lets go of the chair and* **Alec** *comes away with it.*

Sally (*as she holds her father back*)   Come on Dad, sit down, sit down.

Alec *glares at* **Colin**, *but sets down the chair he's won next to* **Sally***'s.* **Sally** *sits on the chair nearest* **Colin**, *and hauls* **Alec** *into the other. Meanwhile,* **Colin** *goes off his side of the stage, and comes back with another chair, which he sits on as before.*

Alec   You're claimed son.

Colin   Fuck you old man.

Sally   Colin! Dad! Come on! We're here to talk about this.

Colin   Tell *him* that!

Sally   I am telling him.

Colin   Radge!

Sally   I'm telling you both. We're here to talk.

Alec   Aye. To talk.

Sally   Well?

Alec (*takes deep breath and starts talking*)   I was happy for the lass when she tellt us she was getting married. What father wouldn't be happy for his daughter? Then she tells me who she's getting married to and Jesus, Colin Grant? Gerry Grant's boy? No way! That family's legion about here, bloody legion so they are.

Sally   British Legion?

Alec   No lass, *bloody* legion. The stories about them are

bloody legion. Everybody kens the Grants! Bloody
thieving bastards! God's sake, and my daughter's going
to marry one of them!

Colin Aye, and she did, so she's a Grant now, so
watch what you say.

Alec Grant might be her name, but it's not her
nature. Grant women, you ken what their nature is:
pure slag, that's what. They'd go on the game but
nobody'd pay them. Drop them for a half of cider and
black. Down on their knees round the back of the
chippie. That's the nature of the Grant women.

Colin You cunt. That's my mother you're talking
about there. (*Stands up.*)

Alec (*looks away*) No it's no.

Colin That's my mother.

Alec No it's no. She's a Geddes, not a Grant. She's
only Grant by name, by marriage just, not birth. A fine
woman, your mother.

Colin (*sits down*) Aye. Fucking aye. And don't you
forget it.

Alec I won't forget it. Rene Geddes. A fine woman.

Sally For God's sake Dad, will you stop going on
about his mother?

Alec Eh?

Sally We're here to talk about us. About me and
Colin. About how he shuts me in the room and won't
let me go out with my mates.

Colin Whores.

Sally About how he gave me that black eye and that.

Colin You were drunk! You fell over the dog!

Sally I did not.

Colin   Ask the dog.

Sally   We're *not* here to talk about his bloody mother.

Alec   Now listen, lass . . .

Sally   Christ, I hear enough about her from him. Mother's chips are this, mother's hoover's that . . . I'm fed up hearing about the old cow.

Rene *strides on from* **Colin**'*s side. She stops after a few steps, points at* **Sally**.

Rene   You . . . shut your filthy gob.

Colin   Mum! What are you doing here?

Rene (*walking towards* **Sally**)   Mouth permanently open, that's always been your problem. Aye, and your legs are the same. (*Leaning over* **Sally**.) Otherwise how else would you have tricked my Colin into marrying you?

Sally *jumps up and slaps* **Rene** *across the face.* **Rene** *goes to hit her back, but* **Alec** *gets in between them, and* **Colin** *leaps over to haul her away. Meanwhile there's shouting along the lines of:*

Rene   Slag, you're a dirty slag.

Sally   Get your hands off me you old cow.

Alec   Ladies, ladies, please.

Colin   Mother, sit down, come on.

After a few seconds' struggle, **Colin** *gets her to sit in his chair, and gets another for himself. They all straighten themselves out.*

Rene   I didn't come here to be hit.

Sally   That's a shame.

Rene   I came cause I want my chance to speak.

Sally   You never miss a chance to do that.

Rene   If youse are all going to be speaking, I want my

say too. It's only fair. All sides of the . . . all sides of the story, ken, they've all got to be heard.

Sally Well what is your side of the story, Rene? Eh? Come on, tell us.

Rene Well . . . I will. But, eh, what are you talking about?

Colin Mother!

Rene I ken, son, but what story is it theday, eh?

Sally We're talking about how your boy's a no-good cheating bastard. How he shuts me in the bedroom with a black eye while he sleeps around the close. Thinks I won't see cause I'm shut up with my eyes puffed out to here. Well I do see! I see!

Alec Listen Sally, listen, can I just say something here?

Sally I seen him!

Alec Aye, and can I tell you what I see?

The lights dim a little and loud music bursts out: 'Same Old Blues' by Freddy King. He stands up, goes to the front of the stage, and stands there as the music plays, staring out front, trying to find a way to articulate what's raging through him. At last, after the first sung verse is finished – about 65 seconds – he speaks, passionately.

Alec I see my daughter upset, and near greeting. And I hate it. Any father would hate it. I tell you folks, I'd rather go blind than see my girl upset. But over the years I've seen it many many times. I've seen her greet when she couldn't get a boyfriend, and then I've seen her greet when she did get one – oh aye. And when that ended . . . well you can picture it. Enough tears to float Edinburgh Castle off its rock. I'd rather go blind than see my daughter greet like that again. I'd rather go blind.

Sally (*stepping forward beside her dad*) This is what hurts.

Not what Colin does to me. But what what-he-does does to my dad. I love my dad. He brought me up himself, and I'm his wee girl still, I ken. His princess. And it's a pain the way he treats me sometimes, that protectiveness, but I ken he does it out of love. And I hate to see him upset. (*Switch:*) But what am I supposed to do? Marry him? It's not possible. And I can't just hang around his house for ever, be his lassie for ever, I've got to get out, see the world for myself, find my own . . . my own . . . *man.*

Alec   Sally . . .

Sally (*shakes her head at dad, turns towards* **Colin**)   Though when you see what you've got yourself into, you wonder. And you wish you couldn't see it. But you do, you do see. And you wish . . . you wish for . . . for anything that isn't this.

Colin (*stepping forward*)   Nobody's perfect. I can see that. I can see she thinks I'm not perfect. Fair enough. But I do, I suppose, love her, ken. Whatever that is. And I ken she loves me too. Whatever. It's just her way of showing it: like her father; jealous, possessive, fucking always sticking her nose in where she'd be better to leave it out. Then she wonders why she sees things she doesn't like. I say to him: keep your nose out of our business, and you won't see your lassie greeting, you'll never see it. And I say to her, have a look at my mother, take a lesson from her: she turned a blind eye to my dad's mistakes, and look what happened: twenty-five years of happy marriage. A good relationship.

Rene (*steps forward, as the music ends*)   CRAP. His father treated me like dirt for twenty-five years. Running around, drinking all the money, keeping me down. Ha. That's what he thought. Well when he was out on the randan, I was enjoying myself too, is that not right Alec?

Alec   Rene, we said we wouldn't talk about that . . .

Rene   Oh aye, he's a fine man, your father, Sally, always has been.

Sally   What are you saying?

Alec   It's a secret.

Colin (*laughs*)   Ho! No secrets today, Alec! No fucking secrets today!

Rene   In this life you've got to take your pleasures when you fucking can, folks. They don't hang around and wait for you to make your mind up. Smash and grab them, that's my motto. Well his father got smashed. And I grabbed Alec. And if you don't like it, you don't have to live it. I have to live this life, and the only way I can make it bearable is smash and grab. And that's all I have to say.

Sally   Well that's a relief.

Rene   Don't start on me you slag! I could tell you a thing or two.

Sally   Oh, here we go.

Rene   I could settle your hash with one word from my mouth.

Sally   Oh aye, and what word might that be, eh? Come on, surprise me. What fucking magic word is that?

Rene   Sorry.

Stunned silence. It lasts a long time: at least fifteen seconds. During it, all four look at **Rene***, and at each other, in astonishment. Eventually,* **Alec** *shakes his head, clears his throat and splutters out:*

Alec   No. No no no. That won't do. No way Rene. You can't just come in here and start lobbing about words like that.

Colin   He's right Mum. I mean look what happened.

The whole fucking thing ground to a halt.

Rene   But I meant it.

Sally   We don't care what you meant, you stupid cow. The fact is there's some things that're just going too far. They just ruin the whole thing for everybody.

Rene   Oh. Sorry.

Alec   Aarrggh!

Colin   Will you stop saying that word!

Rene   Well what the fuck am I meant to say you bunch of cunts?

Sally   That's it.

Rene   Shut the fuck up.

Colin   You tell her Mum. Stupid fucking bitch.

Alec   (*rushing across and grabbing* **Colin**)   You're claimed son.

Sally   (*grabbing both of them, joining in the scuffle*)   Dad! Leave him! Get off!

Rene   (*after looking on for a second or two*)   I can't watch this.

Loud music bursts out, Freddy King's 'Hideaway' again. Simultaneously, the lights go to black.

Methuen Modern Plays
include work by